The Life of St. Rose of Lima—
Illustrated Edition

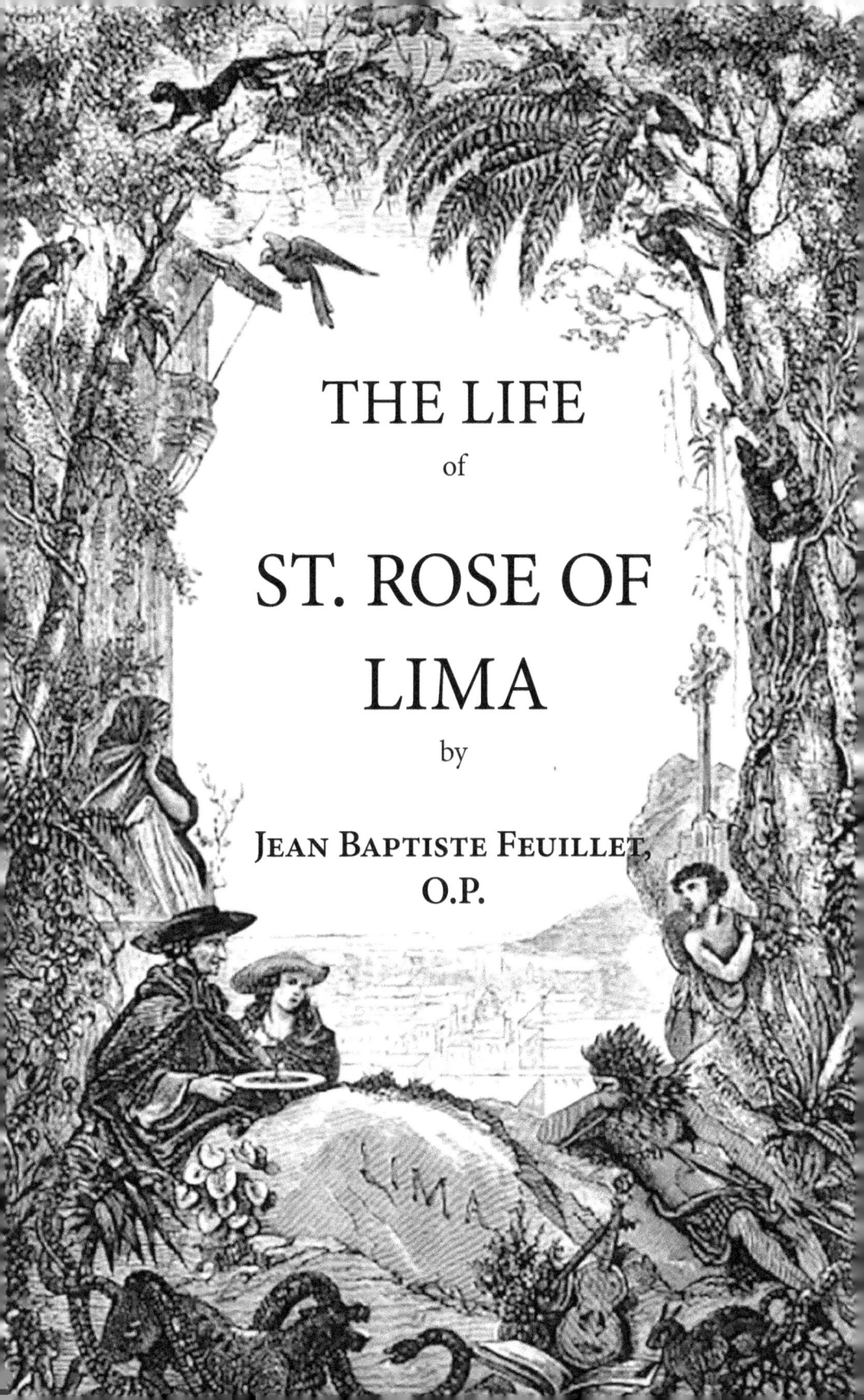

THE LIFE
of
ST. ROSE OF LIMA
by
Jean Baptiste Feuillet, O.P.

This life of St. Rose has been excerpted from *Saints and Servants of God: The Lives of S. Rose of Lima, Bl. Colomba di Rieti, and of S. Juliana Falconieri*, a book that we also publish. That work was originally issued in London by Thomas Richardson and Son in 1863 as part of a series edited by Fr. Frederick Faber of the Oratory, Well worth reading and absorbing, Father Faber's preface is found in that book, but briefly excerpted here so far as it pertains to St. Rose. This derivative edition has been re-typeset and enhanced with seventy-four images. By and large the sketches in her biography taken from Michael A. Fuentes, *Lima, Sketches of the Capital of Peru* are intended to be evocative of Lima as St. Rose would have known it. The persons depicted are therefore types rather than persons known to St. Rose, and while they supply context as they run along the bottom of of the page, they bear little relation to the text.

The several paintings devoted to her go a long way towards capturing her spiritual life and Heavenly destiny, but Lima was–per the sketches–a very earthy place, the place where she nevertheless lived so triumphantly.

Lee M. Gilbert is the editor in 2020.

© 2021 by Arthur M. Gilbert and Son, Publishers. All rights reserved.

www.auldsnu.com

12051 SE 31st Pl, Ste 15
Milwaukie, OR 97222

ISBN 978-0-57884568-5

PRINTED IN THE UNITED STATES OF AMERICA

St. Catherine of Siena, patroness and exemplar of St. Rose

Publishers Note Regarding Her Life

To give the reader some further context for St. Rose's life, she was the daughter of a retired harquebusier in the Spanish Imperial Army, M Gaspar de Flores de la Puente, who was born about 1530 in Extremadura Spain, from which area came also Pizarro, Cortes and de Soto. On May 1st, 1577, he married Maria de Oliva Herrera (1559-1637) in the Sagrario in Lima. S. Rose was the fourth of nine children. She and her siblings in order are:

Gaspar Flores de Oliva 1579-

Bernardina Flores de Oliva 1581-ca 1596

Hernando Flores de Oliva 1584-1627

Isabel (Rose) Flores de Oliva 1586-1617

Francisco Flores de Oliva 1590-

Juana Flores de Oliva 1592-

Antonio Flores de Oliva 1594-

Andres Flores de Oliva 1596-

Francisco Matia Flores de Oliva †

Jacinta Flores de Oliva 1603-

The population of Lima in 1600 was about 26,000. Lima has only 1300 hours of sunshine a year.

During her sojourn there was a relatively enormous presence of religious in Lima. The Dominicans, for example, had 250 friars in their convent, and the Franciscans, Augustinians and Jesuits were also there in large numbers.

St. Turibius of Mogrovejo was her archbishop until she was twenty years old, for he reigned from 1581 to 1606. St. Martin de Porres was also a contemporary and fellow citizen of Lima, for he was born December 9, 1579, in Lima, and he died there November 3, 1639. Although he receives no mention in Feuillet's account, he surely would have been known to her for he was a fellow Dominican and well-known in the city for his charitable works, as was she.

PREFACE

The Life of S. Rose is translated from the French of Father Jean Baptiste Feuillet, a Dominican friar, and Missionary Apostolic in the Antilles; the copy which has been followed is the third edition, published at Paris in 1671, the year of her canonization by Clement X.

English readers, who may not have been in the habit of reading the Lives of the Saints, and especially the authentic Processes of the Congregation of Sacred Rites, may be a little startled with the Life of S. Rose. The visible intermingling of the natural and supernatural worlds, which seems to increase as the saints approach through the grace of God to their first innocence, may even offend where persons have been in the habit of paring and batting down the "unearthly," in order to evade objections and lighten the load of the controversialist, rather than of meditating with awe and thankfulness and deep self-abasement on the wonders of God in His saints, or of really sounding the depths of Christian philosophy, and mastering the principles and general laws which are discernible even in the supernatural regions of hagiology.

The habit of always thinking first how any tenet, or practice, or fact, is most conveniently presentable to an adversary, may soon, and almost imperceptibly, lead to profaneness, by introducing the spirit of rationalism into matters of faith; and to judge from the works of our greatest Catholic divines, it would appear that the deeper theologian a man is, the less does he give way to this studious desire of making difficulties easy at any cost short of denying what is positively de fide. They seem to handle truth religiously just in the way that God is pleased to give it us, rather than to see what they can make of it themselves by shaping it for controversy, and so by dint of skilful manipulation squeeze it through a difficulty. The question is, not "What will men say of this? How will this sound in controversy? Will not this be objected to by heretics?" but, "Is this true? Is this kind of thing approved by the Church? Then what good can I get out of it for my own soul? Ought not my views to be deeper than they are?". . . .

If, then, anyone unaccustomed to the literature of Catholic countries, and with their ears unconsciously untuned by the daily dissonance of the errors and unbelief around them, should be startled by this volume, let him pause before he pronounces judgment. Persons, who have unfortunately more call to defend their religion than time to study it, fancy they gain a sort of mock strength, or at least pleasantly and triumphantly surprise an adversary, when they throw overboard to his mercy, as sailors throw meat to a shark, anything wonderful, as though it were necessarily superstitious. But in this way a man may make wild work of solemn things without knowing it, and he whets rather than stays the appetite of his opponent, who presently follows him up again with a new, and, indeed, in his case, an unanswerable charge of inconsistency. A Catholic, do what he will, cannot weed his religion of the supernatural; and to discriminate between the supernatural and the superstitious is a long work and a hard one, a work of study and of reverent meditation. O how hard it is, if men do not kneel to meditate, to hear a thing denied all round them every day, and yet maintain a joyous and unshaken faith therein! . . .

O in how many may not weak faith be strengthened, and by how many may not dangerous and unsound principles be abandoned, and from how many minds may not stray sympathies with heresy be weeded out, and how many hearts may there not be moved to higher things, to loftier aims, to more heavenly vocations, by this exhibition of the Saints of God! How many are there who by these very Lives have been already won from their tearful wanderings to their Shepherd's fold! and how many more may not God have predestined yet to come the same sweet road under the same gentle compulsion!

F. W. Faber.

St. Wilfrid's,

Feast of Our Lady of Redemption,

1847.

La Merced, a church that S. Rose frequented

CONTENTS

THE LIFE OF S. ROSE OF LIMA

PAGE

CHAPTER I.   1
Her country, her birth, her inclinations, and the vow of virginity which she made at the age of five years

CHAPTER II.   8
Her obedience, the respect she had for her parents, and the assistance she rendered them

CHAPTER III.   14
S. Rose takes the habit of the Third Order of S. Dominic, in imitation of S. Catherine of Siena, whom she had taken for her model

CHAPTER IV.   21
Her humility, her incomparable purity of heart, and other virtues

CHAPTER V.   27
Her fasts, her disciplines, and the other austerities with which she macerated her body

CHAPTER VI.   37
Of the sharp-pointed crown which she wore on her head, and of the hardness of her bed

CHAPTER VII.   46
Of her solitude, and the hermitage which she had built in her father's garden, that she might live quite separated from men

CHAPTER VIII.   53
Jesus Christ espouses the Blessed Rose in the presence of the ever Blessed Virgin

CHAPTER IX.   59

CONTENTS

    Of the close union with God to which she attained by means of mental prayer

CHAPTER X.   65
    She is tormented with interior pains to so frightful a degree, that she is examined by some divines, who declare her state to be from God

CHAPTER XI.   73
    Of the familiar manner in which Jesus Christ, the Blessed Virgin, S. Catherine of Siena, and her Guardian Angel conversed with her; and of the victories which she gained over the devils who tempted her

CHAPTER XII.   83
    Of her invincible patience under persecution, in sickness, and in her other sufferings

CHAPTER XIII.   89
    Of her love for her Divine Spouse Jesus Christ, and of the miracle which she entreated Him to work to inflame the hearts of men with His Divine love

CHAPTER XIV.   98
    Of her devotion towards the most Blessed Sacrament, in defence of which she once prepared herself to suffer martyrdom

CHAPTER XV.   105
    Of her devotion to an image of our Blessed Lady, to the sign of the cross, and to her dear mistress S. Catherine of Siena

CHAPTER XVI.   114
    Of her zeal for the salvation of souls, and her care in assisting the poor in their sickness and necessities

CHAPTER XVII.   125
    Of her confidence in God, and of the protection she received from Him in her necessities

CHAPTER XVIII.   131
    God makes known to S. Rose that a monastery of nuns will be built in Lima, under the name of S. Catherine of Siena, and reveals to her several other secrets

CHAPTER XIX.   137
    Of her last illness and death

CHAPTER XX.   149
    Of the honour which S. Rose received after death, and of the translation of her body, which took place some time afterwards

CHAPTER XXI   162
    Of the revelations which several persons had of the glory of S. Rose

CHAPTER XXII.   167
    Of the miracles which Almighty God worked through the merits of S. Rose

    1. Of the conversions which the prayers of S. Rose obtained

    2. Two dead persons raised to life, and many miraculously cured by touching the body of S. Rose, and invoking her assistance in their infirmities

    3. After S. Rose's death many sick persons were restored to health, and several women assisted in their labour, by touching her veil or some part of her dress.

    4, Several persons afflicted with dysentery, quinsy, fever, frenzy, and other maladies have been miraculously cured by earth from the sepulchre of our Saint.

    5. Pictures of S. Rose applied to persons afflicted with leprosy, quinsy, gout, headache, and other infirmities, have been the means of restoring health to them

CHAPTER XXIII.   192
    Of the efforts made at Rome to obtain from the Pope her canonization

Image Index   200

An harquebusier

THE LIFE OF
SAINT ROSE OF LIMA.

CHAPTER I

HER COUNTRY, HER BIRTH, HER DISPOSITIONS, AND THE VOW OF VIRGINITY WHICH SHE MADE AT THE AGE OF FIVE YEARS

Our blessed Rose, the first spiritual flower which Divine Providence planted and cultivated in the richest part of the New World, was born on the 20th day of April, in the year 1586, at Lima, the capital of Peru in South America. Her father was Gasper Florez, and her mother Mary Oliva, both more considerable by their birth than by their fortune. This virtuous woman, who had been several times in danger of losing her life, by the excessive pains she had endured during her other confinements, was happily preserved from them at the birth of our Saint, who came into the world differently from other children, wrapped up in a double cuticle, like a rose, whose bud is surrounded by leaves as soon as it begins to appear.

The lady Isabel of Herrera, her mother's sister, being

chosen as her godmother, gave her the name of Isabel in baptism; but three months after, as she slept in her cradle, her mother and several other persons, who did not all belong to the family, having perceived on her countenance a beautiful rose, she was called from that time by no other name than Rose, on account of this prodigy.

Her godmother, thinking herself slighted by this change of name, was offended at it, and lived at variance with her sister, till Divine Providence, who watched over the interests of our Saint, put an end to this unhappy dispute, by inspiring his Lordship, the Archbishop of Lima, to give her the name of Rose in confirmation.

Rose, when older, had some scruple about it, on learning that it was not the name she had received in baptism; she thought it was an effect of the complaisance or of the vanity of her parents, who wished to make her beauty more attractive by this agreeable name. Disturbed by this conduct, which she thought unworthy of the spirit of a Christian, she went to the Church of the Friars Preachers; and having entered the Chapel of the Rosary, she cast herself at the feet of the Blessed Virgin, to make known to her her uneasiness. Our Blessed Lady immediately consoled her, assuring her that the name of Rose was pleasing to her Son Jesus Christ and that, as a mark of her affection, she would also honour her with her own name, and that henceforward she should be called Rose of S. Mary. So that we may say, that of all the saints whose names Almighty God has changed by an extraordinary favour, our blessed Rose is the first, and perhaps the only one, whose surname has been also changed by heaven.

Her infancy had a lively resemblance to that of the seraphic saint, Catherine. Never was she troublesome by annoying cries; and never was she seen to shed tears, excepting once, when her nurse had carried her to a neighbouring house, where this sweet child wept, as if to show her sorrow in being taken from her solitude, the sweetness of which she began

to taste, in the house of her father. The holy Fathers teach us, that the just man cannot do or suffer anything virtuously without the help of grace, but that Almighty God works by His grace many wonders in His saints without their co-operation.

This was shown in the blessed Rose, who when only three months old gave proof of a heroic patience: for, some one having thoughtlessly pinched her thumb, by shutting a chest hastily, she concealed the pain it gave her. Her mother having hastened to her at the first news of the accident, she hid the finger, and did not let it appear that she had been hurt. The injury grew worse afterwards from her silence, and violent remedies were necessary, which caused her to lose a part of the nail. The surgeon employed pincers to extract by the roots that part which still remained in the flesh, and was greatly surprised to remark, that, during this painful operation, she did not shed a tear, utter a scream, or even change countenance.

It was not on this occasion alone that she gave proof of her patience; she practised it equally whenever she had anything to suffer. She endured, with an inconceivable constancy, the pain inflicted by cutting off with scissors part of her ear which had become corrupted. At the age of four years she was troubled with a sort of disorder in the head, and her mother, who loved her tenderly, wishing to dress it herself, used a certain powder, so corrosive and burning, that it caused her to shudder from head to foot; still she never complained, though this remedy caused a number of ulcers in her head, which gave her excessive pain.

As coral hardens in the waves, which are the emblem of affliction, so we might say, that the patience of our Saint increased with the greatness of her sufferings; for, during six weeks, the surgeon who attended her cut off every day a portion of flesh, that a new skin might grow in its place, and she suffered this torture with invincible patience.

Almighty God, who designed her to be a living image of His crucified life, did not leave her long without suffering, and He permitted that two years after she should be afflicted with a polyp in her nose, which grew so large that they had recourse to the surgeon to remove it, which he did in three different operations, during which she evinced a super-human patience, suffering this pain with a joy that seemed miraculous, and much resembled that which many martyrs have shown in the dreadful torments inflicted upon them by their executioners.

This early apprenticeship in the school of Calvary, where she learned from Jesus Christ Crucified, to suffer all sorts of pains and afflictions, disposed our young Rose to offer to God, from her infancy, the agreeable odour of the ardent charity with which her heart was inflamed.

She received most happily the first rays of Divine grace, and her little brother contributed to this; for playing near her one day, he threw accidentally a quantity of mud on her hair. Being naturally neat, she was vexed at his carelessness, and was on the point of going away; when he said to her with a gravity beyond his years, "My dear sister, do not be angry at this accident, for the curled ringlets of girls are hellish cords, which bind the hearts of men, and miserably draw them into eternal flames."

Rose received these words, which he uttered with the zeal of a preacher, as an oracle from Heaven: she entered into herself, and renouncing for ever the vanities of the world, she gave herself entirely to God, and conceived an extreme horror for sin. From that time she felt herself powerfully drawn to prayer; and she applied herself to it so assiduously, that she was not content with giving to it part of the day, and the greatest part of the night; we may even say, that sleep was no interruption to her prayer, for her imagination represented to her during her repose the absorbing idea she had formed to herself of her Divine Spouse in the fervour of her prayers, and of her converse with Him during the day.

In this sacred intercourse she received a lively inspiration

from Almighty God to follow in the footsteps of S. Catherine of Siena, by a perfect imitation of the virtues of this seraphic lover of God. And because virginity, joined to baptismal innocence and to the flower of youth, is a double lily, which sheds its splendour on the spouses of Jesus Christ; so Rose, moved by the spirit of God, consecrated to Him irrevocably and by vow, at the age of five years, her virginal purity, by the promise she gave Him never to have any other Spouse but Him alone. Thus we may say of S .Rose, what S. Ambrose said of S. Agnes, that her piety and virtue were above her years, and beyond the strength of nature.

As soon as she had made this vow, she cut off her hair, unknown to her mother, in order to manifest to the Spouse she had chosen, that by thus disfiguring herself she intended rather to disgust than to please men; and that she absolutely renounced the world, with which she never wished to have any intercourse. We learn from the testimony of her confessors, that she began to have the use of reason when this heavenly ardour filled her soul; and this generous action was so pleasing to Almighty God, that He showered down upon her His choicest benedictions, and enriched her with so many graces, that she preserved her baptismal innocence till her death.

The cathedral of Lima and its Sagrario where Gaspar Flores and María de Oliva y Herrera were married

CHAPTER II

HER OBEDIENCE, THE RESPECT SHE HAD FOR HER PARENTS, AND THE ASSISTANCE SHE RENDERED THEM.

To obey the parents from whom we have received our life, is only the effect of an ordinary degree of virtue; and there would have been nothing remarkable in the obedience of the blessed Rose, if she had contented herself with simply fulfilling this duty; but she infinitely increased its merit by perfectly complying with that which she owed to her parents, without failing to accomplish what Almighty God required of her. She managed so well, that she executed whatever her father and mother commanded her, without omitting the least part of her duty towards God. Her mother, like many others who love their children more for the world than for heaven, often begged her to take care of her beauty, and even desired her to use cosmetics and paint to preserve its freshness; but Rose, who knew this to be contrary to modesty and simplicity, which are the only ornaments of Christian beauty, entreated her so earnestly not to oblige her to do this, and not to imitate these mothers who sacrifice the salvation of their children to their own ambition, that she, by degrees, induced her to think differently; thus making the law of the spirit victorious over that of the flesh, and causing the secret aversion with which her Divine Spouse inspired her for this worldly custom, to triumph over the unjust command she had received to conform to it.

Another time her mother made her wear a garland of flowers on her head. Not thinking herself strong enough to effect a change in this command, she obeyed; but she sanctified her submission by the painful mortification with which she accompanied it: for God having brought to her mind the remembrance of the cruel thorns which had composed His crown in His Passion, she took the garland, and fixed it on her head with a large needle, which she plunged so deeply into her head, that it could not be drawn out without the help of a surgeon, who had much difficulty in doing it. Thus she contrived to elude without resisting the orders of her mother, when they were openly opposed to the law of God, and she punished herself severely when she obeyed her in anything that partook of the vanity of the world. This fidelity was most pleasing to her Divine Spouse, and she perceived by a remarkable circumstance, that she could not in the least depart from it without offending Him.

One day, having put on a pair of scented gloves in order to oblige her mother, she had no sooner begun to wear them than her hands became cold and benumbed, and soon after she felt in them so violent a heat, that notwithstanding the love of our Saint for suffering, she was obliged to take off the gloves, which caused this torture; and God, to show the blessed Rose that the little breath of vanity which had induced her, under the specious pretext of obedience, to wear these gloves, had inflamed the zeal of her Divine Spouse, showed her the same gloves in the night surrounded by flames. From that time she never obeyed her mother in anything that was agreeable to the world or to nature, without joining some act of mortification to her obedience. Her mother having absolutely commanded her to remove the pieces of wood which she had secretly put into her pillow, she did so; but she put in their place so great a quantity of wool, and stuffed it in such a manner, that her pillow, from its hardness, might have been taken for a log of wood covered with linen.

The stratagem which she practised in order to avoid appearing at assemblies, or accompanying her mother in the visits she paid to her friends and relations, was not less surprising; for she rubbed her eyelids with pimento, which is a very sharp burning sort of Indian pepper: by this means she escaped going into company, for it made her eyes red as fire, full of tears, and so painful, that she could not bear the light. Her mother having found out this artifice, reprimanded her for it, and mentioned the example of Ferdinand Perez, who had lost his sight by a similar act of indiscretion; Rose answered modestly, "It would be much better for me, my dear mother, to be blind all the rest of my life, than to be obliged to see the vanities and follies of the world."

After this answer, her mother seeing clearly that it was a repugnance for these visits, and for the dress she was compelled to wear on these occasions, which caused her to inflict this pain on herself, no longer urged her to accompany her, and allowed her to dress as she liked, in a poor stuff dress, which she wore with great satisfaction, for she sought nothing but contempt and abjection. In all indifferent things S. Rose obeyed willingly, and never received a command from her mother which she did not cheerfully fulfil. Her mother wishing one day to try her obedience, ordered her to embroider some flowers in the wrong way: Rose obeyed blindly, and spoiled her work, and her mother, feigning to be angry, reproved her for it. This truly obedient daughter answered, that she had perceived that her work was good for nothing, but had not dared to disobey the order given her; that it was of no consequence to her in what manner she traced a flower, but that she could not fail in obedience to her mother's orders. For this reason she never began her work without asking her mother's leave, and she told one of her friends, who seemed astonished at it, that she did it expressly to join to her work the merit of obedience.

Her obedience did not concern her mother only, to whom she was so submissive that she never drank without her permission, and dared not begin her work without her express order: it extended even to the servant of the house, whom she respected as her mistress, and whom she obeyed always joyfully, particularly when she was cross and ill-tempered.

Her mother, who was of a bilious temperament and often angry, sometimes forbade her to drink; and as she did not know that her virtuous daughter never would drink without her permission, Rose was often known to pass six days without drinking. Her parents having taken her to Canta, a very unhealthy part of the country, she was seized with a contraction of the nerves in her hands and feet, and as this arose from cold her mother made her wear skins, the hair of which was very irritating, and desired her not to take them off. Rose bore with them for several days, without mentioning the insupportable heat they caused, that she might not be wanting in obedience; but her hands and feet became so inflamed in consequence, that numbers of little blisters were formed in them, which afterwards became very painful ulcers.

Obedience generally terminates with life, but the blessed Rose manifested it even when in her tomb. The mother prioress of the Convent of Nuns of S. Dominic at Lima, commanded the picture of Rose, in virtue of the obedience which every one in the house owed to her, to enable them to find a silver spoon which a servant belonging to the monastery had lost, that they might avoid any rash judgment of innocent persons; and as if our Saint had animated the colours of her picture with that spirit of obedience, which had made her so submissive to God, and to His creatures for His love, the prioress perceived immediately on the table the lost spoon, and we might say, that the picture placed it there, to represent the perfect obedience of its original.

Who could express her exact obedience to her parents

during her whole life, her respect and the tender love she bore them? At the times when she was suffering most from weakness, she generally spent more than half the night in working to help them in their necessities, and though she devoted twelve hours every day to mental prayer, she did more work than another, who had less to do, would have done in four days, and her work had so much beauty and delicacy that it seemed to surpass art and nature.

She was a perfect mistress of needlework, either in designing flowers or executing them in embroidery or in tapestry; and what is surprising is, that though her mind was often elevated to God and absorbed in the contemplation of His perfections while she was working, yet her hand guided her work as perfectly as if her mind were solely intent upon it.

Besides her needlework she cultivated a little garden, in which she grew violets and other flowers, which she sold to help her parents in their necessities; and as all her industry was insufficient to save them from poverty, she confessed ingenuously to a great servant of God, that Jesus Christ her Divine Spouse supplied the deficiency by secret and wonderful means. She tended them in sickness with incredible assiduity; she was always at their bedside, she passed days and nights there, and only left them to perform for them elsewhere some other service. She made their bed, prepared their medicine, and was ready by day and by night to perform for them the vilest and most difficult services.

I must not conclude this chapter without speaking of the ineffable joy she procured for her mother-who would otherwise have been overwhelmed with grief, in seeing her depart out of this life. This blessed Saint, when on her death-bed, foreseeing the anguish her mother would feel at her death, earnestly begged her Divine Spouse to console her in this affliction; and He did so by bestowing upon her so great a plenitude of joy, that she juridically deposed that she felt an extraordinary joy when this death took place, which would otherwise have drawn from her abundance of tears and sighs. She further testified, that this favour not only rendered her insensible to this great loss, but took possession of her mind so powerfully, that for several days she could scarcely bear its violence, and that Almighty God had shown her, by this experience, the happiness which her holy daughter enjoyed in heaven, and the torrent of delights which He poured out upon her soul in that happy abode.

San Sebastian, where S. Rose was baptized

CHAPTER III

S. ROSE TAKES THE HABIT OF THE THIRD ORDER OF S. DOMINIC, IN IMITATION OF S. CATHERINE OF SIENA, WHOM SHE HAD TAKEN FOR HER MODEL.

If anyone should attempt to compare the lives of S. Catherine of Siena and of S. Rose, he would find so great a resemblance between these two lovers of the Son of God, that he would have some difficulty in discovering whether this sweet flower sprang forth in the Indies, or whether it was transplanted from Italy into Peru; for in S. Rose all the characteristics of S. Catherine of Siena were to be seen, the same manner of living, the same inclinations, the same favours from God, and so great a similarity in figure and countenance, that one might easily have been taken for the other.

S. Rose having cut off her hair after making her vow of virginity, seemed thereby to have deprived anyone who might seek her in marriage of the hope of succeeding in this design. But the advantages she had received from nature, offered an innocent opposition to the resolution she had made to preserve until death the precious lily of her virginity; for her extreme beauty, the refinement of her mind, her delightful conversation, and her virtue itself, captivated many hearts by their charms, and drew towards her admirers from all parts.

In order to extinguish these rising flames in the hearts of others, she invented all sorts of means to disfigure herself;

S. Rose rejects a suitor

she made her face pale and livid with fasting, she sought to destroy her delicate white complexion, she washed her hands in hot lime to take the skin off them; and to prevent others from feeling any pleasure to which the sight of her might give rise, she shut herself up closely in the house, and went out but very seldom, and when it was quite necessary; and having been taken to Canta, a little village near one of the most celebrated mines in Peru, she remained there four entire years without leaving the house; she would not even go to see a beautiful garden, close to the door of the house where she lived, from which she might have easily viewed these famous machines called moles, for which Peru is renowned.

Notwithstanding all these precautions, she was not able to prevent several persons from seeking her in marriage. Amongst others, one of the most distinguished ladies in the city, as much delighted with her virtue as with her beauty, wished her only son to marry her; she openly made the request to S. Rose's parents, who having eleven children to provide for, received the proposal most favourably, thinking the alliance would be very advantageous to their family.

Rose was the only person to whom this offer was disagreeable; she blamed herself for it, and that frail beauty which brought upon her this great misfortune; and seeing that there was no means of escaping, but by openly declaring that she would never consent to marry, having a horror of the very thought of it, she made known her resolution with a firmness which surprised her parents, though it did not make them give up the hope of inducing her to comply with their wishes. They employed threats and caresses, and seeing her inflexible in her resolutions, they tried the effects of ill-treatment, they gave her blows, and loaded her with injuries; in a word, S. Rose had the same sufferings to endure, as were inflicted on S. Catherine of Siena by her mother, for a similar reason.

After this storm, she sought in the third order of S. Dominic, a port where she might be secure all the rest of her life from the furious tempests which the devil would be sure to raise against her purity as long as she remained in the world. When her resolution was known, the nuns of the most celebrated monasteries in Lima wished her to take their habit. Monsignor Turibius, the Archbishop of Lima, requested her to enter a convent of S. Clare, which his niece, Mary de Quignonez, had just finished building, that thus she might be the foundation-stone of the holy edifice; but Rose, who, from the age of five years, had proposed to herself S. Catherine of Siena as the model for her imitation, thought it was not sufficient to copy her innocence and her other virtues, but that she must embrace the same state of life, which would not prevent her from continuing to assist her parents.

St. Turibius of Mogrovejo

Almighty God confirmed her in this resolution by two miracles. The first took place when she had the intention of going to the Monastery of the Incarnation, where the nuns were anxiously expecting her. Before setting out she went to bid farewell to our Blessed Lady in the Chapel of the Rosary, belonging to the convent of S. Dominic, and there remained immovable on her knees at the foot of the altar; when her prayer was finished, although she made several efforts to rise, she could not succeed; she called her brother, who was in the church, to her assistance; he took her hand, and pulled her violently without being able to move her from the spot; this appearing to her to be a sign from heaven, she resolved not to prosecute her design, but to return home. She had no sooner come to this determination than she was able to rise and leave the chapel without difficulty.

Almighty God showed her by another miracle that He would have her choose the order of Friars Preachers in preference to any other, in imitation of S. Catherine of Siena, who was one of its brightest ornaments. Amongst the almost innumerable quantity of differently coloured butterflies which are to be seen in Lima, one, prettily marked with white and black, the colours of the habit of S. Dominic's order, came and fluttered round her; she considered this as a heavenly indication that she was to accomplish the design she had formerly conceived of becoming a religious in the third order of this great patriarch. She received the habit solemnly at the age of twenty years from the hands of the Rev. Father Alphonso Velasquez, on the 10th day of August, 1606, with much satisfaction; but she would have quitted it before her profession for three reasons, if she had not been specially guided by Almighty God, whose will it was that she should remain in the order of S. Dominic.

In the first place, Don Gonzalez, a very great benefactor of hers, and who possessed great influence over her mind, pressed her earnestly to become a discalced Carmelite, offering to procure her the necessary portion, and assigning as his reason that a cloistered life was more suitable to her than remaining with her parents amid the bustle of the world.

Secondly, she thought that as she wore a white habit this dress required greater innocence than hers; and that as her life did not come up to the perfection of this new state, she was deceiving the world by a false appearance of virtue under this holy habit.

Thirdly, as she had only quitted her secular dress that she might live unknown and forgotten by men, she was surprised to find that her new state of a religious person, instead of

SHE BECOMES A DOMINICAN

keeping her concealed, showed her forth as a light in the House of God, and that her reputation was so universally diffused through the town, that she was the only subject of conversation, was pointed out in the streets, distinguished from others, and praised by every one. Her modesty suffered inconceivable pain from these praises, especially when she knew that some pious persons, from the high esteem they had of her virtue, did not hesitate to compare her to S. Catherine of Siena. Though these applauses gave her so much pain, she still persevered in wearing the habit she had obtained from heaven by so many signs; for having conceived the design of quitting it in order to live more concealed, she went to kneel before the altar of the Holy Rosary to visit the Blessed Virgin, her usual refuge in the hour of distress, and as soon as she began her prayer she became sweetly insensible. These who were in the chapel concluded immediately that she was in a rapture, and,

She takes the Dominican habit

observing her closely, they remarked that her countenance changed, being first pale, and then becoming fiery, and so luminous that it sent forth rays of brightness on every side. When she came to herself after this ecstasy, she made known by the words which she poured forth from the abundance of her heart, that Almighty God had confirmed her entrance into that holy order, and that she was resolved to live and die in it.

S. Dominic de Guzman as Penitent

CHAPTER IV

HER HUMILITY, HER INCOMPARABLE PURITY OF HEART, AND OTHER VIRTUES.

Humility, which the holy fathers have always considered as the foundation of the other Christian virtues, was so deeply rooted in the soul of S. Rose, that her labours seem to have been directed all her life to the contempt of herself, and to the practice of every sort of humiliation and abjection.

To satisfy this predominant inclination of her heart, she did not find it sufficient to choose as her employment the vilest occupations of the house, she considered herself infinitely below the servant; and this sentiment of her miseries and unworthiness induced her often to cast herself at the feet of a poor country girl named Marianne, who worked in the house, and entreat her earnestly to strike her, to spit upon her, to trample her under foot, and to treat her as the most abject and contemptible creature in the world. When she received blows or harsh words on account of the retired life she led, she thought she well deserved them, and that by her own fault she had brought on herself this injurious treatment, and she suffered it with humility and patience. When any misfortune happened to the country or to her family, she attributed it to her sins, which had drawn down this chastisement from heaven; and her humility made her usually say that she was a burden, useless to the world and odious to nature; that she was unworthy to see the light; that she was a sink of corruption infecting the air; and that she was surprised that Almighty God did not cause the earth to open and swallow up so unhappy a creature, who for her enormous offences deserved to be annihilated.

As she was deeply penetrated with a sense of her own nothingness and misery, it was to her an insupportable cross to see herself honoured; her humility could not bear to hear a word of praise; and on this account hearing one day Michael Garrez, canon of the cathedral of Lima, who had come to visit Don Gonzalez, her intimate friend, praising her in the course of the conversation, and extolling the favours she had received from Almighty God, she retired into her chamber, where she began to strike her breast, to weep and to groan in the presence of God; and to punish herself for giving, as she thought, a false opinion of herself to men, she gave herself several violent blows on the head, to force in more deeply the iron points of the crown which she always wore concealed under her veil.

Having once performed an heroic act of virtue in something very difficult and repugnant to nature, the wife of Don Gonzalez, fearing that she would injure her health very much by these laborious works, spoke to her confessor, the Rev. Father Alphonso Velasquez, and begged him to reprimand her severely for it, and to forbid her to attempt works of piety beyond her strength. He followed this advice, reproving her for her action, and desiring her to perform nothing extraordinary, capable of injuring her health. S. Rose received this reproof respectfully, rejoicing before God to see herself despised, and to find humiliation in these acts of virtue from which she had so much reason to fear vain-glory and the esteem of men.

During the three last years of her life, which she spent with Don Gonzalez, she obeyed his children, and all his servants; she did nothing without his express permission; and her humility often made her ask on her knees for a little water for the love of God, like a beggar, whose only means of subsistence is from the alms given him. In the time of sickness she usually concealed the greater part of her sufferings; but when her symptoms and weakness made them evident, she spoke of them as the just reward of her sins; and when she made known the insupportable pains she endured in every part of her body, she did so to make others consider her as an abominable sinner, whom Almighty God chastised thus rigorously in punishment of the crimes she had committed.

She was not only thoroughly persuaded herself, that she was infinitely guilty in the sight of Almighty God; but scarcely anyone else, who saw her at confession, and witnessed the abundance of tears she shed at the feet of the priest, and heard the half-stifled sobs to which her contrite heart gave vent, would have failed to take her for some public sinner, doing penance for her crimes. Yet she never committed one single sin capable of destroying the grace of God in her soul. She led so pure and innocent a life that her confessors had often great difficulty in finding matter for absolution in these things of which she accused herself with so many tears.

She kept so strict a watch over herself, that she was never heard to speak one word louder than another, or to find the least fault with the conduct or actions of others. There was nothing in her behaviour that could give annoyance to these with whom charity or duty obliged her to converse; on the contrary, her sweet and obliging manners made her so agreeable to every one, that it was commonly said, that the name of "Rose" did not suit her, because she had not its thorns.

Her charity towards mankind was so universal that this queen of the virtues seemed to be the soul which animated her words, her actions, and her whole conduct. This love which she had for God and her neighbour filled her whole heart, and had so entirely disengaged it from earthly things, that she was insensible to the pleasures which most men love so passionately. Being asked one day if, in the midst of the

The Church of S. Agustin, one of several S. Rose visited frequently.

delights and consolations which Almighty God infused abundantly into her soul, she did not feel her heart attached to worldly things, she confessed that it was impossible for her to think of them, or to take the least pleasure in them.

By this detachment from creatures, she attained to a purity of heart, in some degree similar to that which the angels possess by the privilege of their nature; for during the course of her life, which lasted thirty-one years, she never was guilty of any venial sin of impurity; and, what is quite miraculous, she was never assailed with impure thoughts, from which even the most cherished and favoured saints of God have not been exempt. Eleven learned religious, six of the order of Friars Preachers, and five Jesuits, who have several times heard her general confessions, have deposed this on their oath.

After her face had become emaciated, and had lost its beauty from the effects of fasting, penances, and cold water, which she poured so abundantly over her body that she nearly extinguished its natural heat, every one seeing the condition to which her austerities had reduced her, held her in greater veneration than ever; and she was considered in Lima as a living image of the penitential life led by the anchorites who have sanctified the deserts by their great mortifications. As her humility feared nothing so much as this universal esteem, and her modesty suffered greatly from these applauses, she had recourse to prayer, to put an end to the cause of them; and she obtained by her prayers the restoration of the brightness of her eyes, and of that brilliant complexion which her austerities had destroyed, so that she became as fresh and beautiful as before; and it happened, one Good Friday, as she was returning home from the church at noon, with a colour on her cheeks that heightened the beauty which Almighty God had given back to her, some young libertines who saw her pass, surprised to see her looking so well, railed at her for it, as if she were returning from some feast, where she had been enjoying herself, and insolently asked her, if that were the manner in which devout people fasted; yet she had fasted all Lent, on orange pippins and water, and had just spent thirty hours in tears, prayers, and groans in the church of S. Dominic, without eating or drinking.

She was still more careful to hide from the eyes of men the spiritual graces and favours she received from God, and fearing they might be perceived in spite of all the precautions she took to keep them secret, she earnestly begged Him from her infancy, not to allow the graces He bestowed upon her to be known by men; and this having been granted by her Divine Spouse, we may easily believe that she kept to herself the greatest part of the extraordinary things that passed in her interior, and that her directors were only made acquainted with the least part of the graces she received from heaven.

We cannot be surprised at this, since the blessed Spirits, taking the part of her modesty, assisted her to hide her virtues, as is shown in the following example. One day, when she was at church, she remembered having left her discipline on her table, and as her door did not shut, she was seized with great apprehension, that some one belonging to the house would perceive this dear instrument of penance. In this uneasiness, she formed a wish within herself, that the Blessed Virgin would put it in a certain place in her room, which she interiorly pointed out to her. Returning home, she did not find her discipline where she had left it, but saw to her astonishment, that this sweet and compassionate Queen of Heaven, to satisfy her desire, and take away her fear, had shut it up in the place which she had thought of.

CHAPTER V

HER FASTS, HER DISCIPLINES, AND THE OTHER AUSTERITIES WITH WHICH SHE MACERATED HER BODY.

All the graces which Christians receive, being derived from the torn and wounded Heart of the Son of God, inspire them with a love of sufferings, and make them practise austerities so frightful, that their innocent excess in the use of them can only be excused by the necessity which baptism imposes, of dying with Him on the cross in order to reign with Him in heaven; for they know that their predestination to eternal happiness includes these mortifications, which are to assimilate them to Jesus Christ, their Head; for this reason S. Paul considers this spirit of penance in Christians, as the special characteristic of their sanctity, when he says that they that are Christ's crucify the flesh, with its vices and concupiscences.

This love of the cross was so ardent in the soul of S. Rose, that the reader would scarcely give credit to that part of her life which treats of her fasts and other mortifications, if we could not assure him, that all which is related has been taken from the juridical informations of the examination, made by the Pope's express order, that he might proceed to her beatification.

She arrived at an astonishing degree of abstinence, by the same means which S. Catherine of Siena employed. From her

S. Rose as penitent

infancy she abstained from all sorts of fruits, which are delicious in Peru. At six years of age she began to fast, three days a week, on bread and water. At fifteen she made a vow never to eat meat, unless she were obliged by these who had authority over her, and whom she thought she could not disobey without sin. When her mother took her with her to dine with some ladies of rank, who invited them out of devotion, and obliged her to eat meat at their table, her obedience caused her a pain in the chest, which brought on fever and other dangerous symptoms.

The same thing happened when meat was ordered for her by physicians: and so far was it from doing her any good, that it always made her relapse into a more dangerous state. The most expeditious method of relieving and curing her on these occasions, was to give her a piece of brown bread soaked in water; and experience proved, in several instances, that this diet restored her to her original health. Her mother, who only looked upon her with the eyes of flesh and blood, seeing her face pale and disfigured, blamed her conduct, and even wished to persuade her that she committed a mortal sin, by thus denying herself the necessary nourishment for the preservation of life. To prevent her from continuing this manner of living, she obliged her to sit at table with the rest of the family, but this enlightened daughter contrived to elude her vigilance, by begging the servant to offer her only a sort of dish made without salt, composed of a crust of coarse bread, and a handful of very bitter herbs. This food was so bad and disagreeable, that she found a voluntary mortification at the same table where others sought to gratify their appetites. She was accustomed herself to gather wild herbs in the forest, and to cultivate them carefully in her garden, that she might have the materials for her self-denial always ready at hand.

She hid under the largest tufts of these plants a vessel full of sheep's gall, with which she sprinkled her food, and washed her mouth every morning. One of her favourite repasts, which seemed to her the most delicious, as it was the bitterest, was to eat the leaves of that creeping plant, the granadille, whose flowers represent so perfectly the crown of thorns, the nails, the pillar, and the other instruments of the Passion of the Son of God, that it is commonly called the " Passion Flower" in Europe: so that we can scarcely tell whether eating or abstinence was the greatest mortification to her. Her fast was so severe and rigorous, that in twenty-four hours she took nothing but a piece of bread and a little water. These who have visited America, and felt its burning heats, will acknowledge that our Saint suffered by these austere fasts a martyrdom of which we can have no idea; for the extreme heat that prevails in that burning climate exhausts the strength so much, that it is necessary to eat frequently, as a preservative against weakness.

She had accustomed herself to fast in this manner, especially the few last years of her life; she observed very exactly the seven months' fast of her order, from the festival of the Exaltation of the Holy Cross till Easter. From the beginning of Lent, she left off bread, contenting herself with a few orange pippins every day of the forty that are consecrated to penance; on Fridays she took only five; during the rest of the year, she eat so little, that what she took in eight days was scarcely sufficient nourishment for twenty-four hours.

She was known to make a moderate sized loaf and a pitcher of water last fifty days. One time she remained seven weeks without drinking a drop of water or any other liquor; and towards the end of her life she very often passed several successive days without eating or drinking. She frequently shut herself up on Thursday in her oratory, and remained there till Saturday without food or sleep, and so completely absorbed in God in a sort of ecstasy, that she continued there immovable, and as if incapable of rising from the place where she was praying on her knees. She once passed eight entire days without any food but the bread of angels which she received in the holy communion; and her supernatural abstinence was so well known to all the inhabitants of Lima, that they were aware that she passed weeks without eating or drinking, and that when necessity compelled her to drink a little water to assuage the burning heat which consumed her, she took it warm, to mortify sensuality in the pleasure she might have felt from drinking cold water.

That which seems miraculous in her austerities is, that our Saint derived more strength from her fasts than from the nourishment she took; for while she deprived herself of natural food, she imbibed from the sacred Wound of the adorable Heart of Jesus Christ, like S. Catherine of Siena, a delicious nectar which strengthened her more efficaciously than the most solid nourishment could have done.

It was no less astonishing that she could find room on her emaciated body to engrave in it by her disciplines the wounds of the Son of God; and that she should have been able to draw from it these streams of blood which she every day caused to flow; with iron chains and her other instruments of penance, she practised such terrible austerities that her confessors were obliged to restrict her in the use of them. After she became a nun she was not content with a common sort of discipline; she made one for herself of two iron chains, with which she gave herself such blows every night, that her blood sprinkled the walls and made a stream in the middle of the room, so prodigious a quantity did she draw from her veins. She disciplined herself in this manner seven times; first, for her own sins; secondly, for souls engaged in sin; thirdly, for the pressing necessities of the Church; fourthly, when Peru or Lima were threatened with some great misfortune; fifthly, for the souls in purgatory; sixthly, for these in their agony; seventhly, in reparation of the outrages offered to God.

The people of Lima, having one day misunderstood the meaning of the words addressed to them by Father Solano, a celebrated Franciscan preacher, thought he said that the earth was going to open and swallow up the town in a few days; in consequence of this mistake the whole place was thrown into consternation. Rose, taking pity on the terrified people, retired to her oratory, and to appease the anger of God she took the discipline so severely that she was nearly dying in consequence.

As she practised this penance every night, she reopened her bleeding wounds by making new ones; and being careful to prolong her suffering, she contrived not to strike always in the same place; but she reiterated her blows so frequently that she did not allow her wounds time to close; scarcely did they begin to heal than she opened them again by fresh blows; thus her whole body was almost one entire wound.

These in the house who heard the sound of the blows she inflicted on herself had a horror of this cruel treatment, and were, at the same time, touched with pity for this innocent penitent, who felt none for herself. Father John of Laurenzana, her confessor, being informed of the manner in which she treated her body, commanded her to use moderation; she obeyed, but she begged so earnestly, that he could not refuse her the permission she asked to take five thousand more stripes in the course of three or four days. She had shown from her infancy the first sparks of that fire which inflamed her soul with the love of penance; for when she was only five years old she carried through mortification heavy tiles and stumps of trees from one place to another with great difficulty. She entreated Marianne the servant, and the dear confidant of her austerities, to load her with heavy stones in the corner where she usually prayed; and she heaped upon her so great a quantity sometimes, that Rose, overcome with the weight of this burden, fell fainting and half dead to the ground. When she was fourteen, she used to leave her room at night when every one in the house had retired to rest, and walk about barefooted in the garden, carrying a long and heavy cross on her wounded shoulders; the joy which she felt under this beloved burden rendering her insensible to the effects of the air and the season.

Her confessor having ordered her to use an ordinary discipline and leave off her iron chain, she made it into three rows, and wore it round her body, and after passing the ends through the ring of a padlock, she threw the key into a corner, where it would have been very difficult to find it. This chain very soon took the skin off, and entered so deeply into her flesh that it was no longer visible; and one night she felt so terrible a pain from it, that she fainted and was near dying. The servant having awoke at a cry she uttered, quickly ran to her assistance. Rose, seeing herself obliged to confess the truth, begged her to help her to take off the chain, before her mother, awakened by the noise, should come up to her room. Marianne found no other means than by breaking the padlock; but they could not do this, and she was obliged to

go down to the garden for a stone to break it. While she was gone, Rose, fearing her mother would surprise them, had recourse to prayer, which served as a key to open the lock, for Marianne, entering with her stone, saw the padlock open of itself and separate from the links of the chains; thus they succeeded in taking it off, though not without causing great pain and an abundant effusion of blood. Her wounds were no sooner healed than she put the chain on again; but as soon as it had entered into her flesh, her confessor ordered her to send it to him, and in obeying him she suffered the same pain and loss of blood as before. After her death, Mary of Usategni, kept some links of this bloody chain, which exhaled so sweet an odour that every one who smelt it was obliged to confess it to be supernatural.

She bound her arms from the shoulder to the elbow with thick cords, which caused her great pain by compressing tightly the muscles of this fleshy part. In order to suffer more she rubbed herself with nettles, making her body one entire blister, and with thorns, which, entering deeply into the flesh, drew forth quantities of blood. She used two hair-shirts; the first, being only two feet long, did not satisfy her desire of suffering; nevertheless, she used it till she obtained another, woven of horsehair, with two sleeves, and which hung from her shoulders to her knees. She appeared yet more glorious in the eyes of God when wearing this strange coat of arms, from her having armed it underneath with a great quantity of points of needles, to increase her excessive sufferings by this ingenious cruelty. She wore this frightful hair-shirt several years with incredible joy, and she only quitted it by the express order of her confessor, when a vomiting of blood came on.

As she was insatiable of pain, seeing her hair-shirt taken from her, she chose a sack of the coarsest stuff she could find, and made it neatly in the form of a shift. It would be impossible to express the suffering this rough dress caused her; sometimes it made the perspiration stream from her in great drops; sometimes she fell fainting under it, and was unable to take a step without great torture. These austerities were insufficient to satisfy her thirst for suffering: she watched also for the hour in which cooking was going on in the house, and, when no one could see her, she exposed the soles of her feet to the heat at the mouth of the oven, where it is the greatest, that no part of her body might be without a wound, and she kept them there till the pain of her half-roasted feet quite overcame her.

This was the treatment our Saint inflicted on her innocent body, though her frequent attacks of illness gave her plenty of occasions of suffering. She would have practised yet greater and more cruel mortifications if her confessors had not prevented her. What astonishes us in her conduct is, that she suspended the interior joy with which Almighty God favoured her in her greatest sufferings, for fear that this spiritual sweetness might extend to her body, and that by making it participate in the delight of her soul her insupportable sufferings would be softened. We may, therefore say that her pains were unmixed with any consolation; they resembled, in a manner till then unknown, these suffered by the Son of God in His Passion, during which He never permitted the superior part of His soul, which was sovereignly happy, to communicate any part of its happiness to its afflicted body. We consider this divorce of the flesh and the spirit in our Saint, as one of the great wonders that have made her the admiration of the Peruvian people. When charity induced some pious persons to exhort her to moderate her austerities, she answered, "As I cannot do any good, is it not just that I should suffer whatever I am capable of enduring?'

The Rimac, which divides Lima

CHAPTER VI

OF THE SHARP-POINTED CROWN WHICH SHE WORE AND OF THE HARDNESS OF HER BED.

THE saints being predestinated to resemble the Son of God in His state of sacrifice and immolation on the cross, according to S. Paul, who makes their greatness consist in this conformity, "whom He predestinated to be made conformable to the image of His Son," every one will allow that a crown of thorns on the head of the blessed Rose was necessary to render her a perfect image of Jesus crucified, and that the portrait would not have been faithful had it not represented the bloody thorns which crowned the head of her Divine Spouse, and which were the dearest object of her thoughts.

To copy it in reality, when very young she made herself a crown of pewter, studded with little sharp- pointed nails; she put it generously on her head without fearing the pain it would inevitably cause her. She wore it several years, but only as a preparation for a more cruel one, in which she fixed ninety-nine iron points; she wore, this during the ten last years of her life; and it furnished her with a still greater occasion of exercising her love, and her patience, for considering the crown of thorns of Jesus Christ on the head of S. Catherine of Siena, she thought she might obtain the same favour. In this ardent desire of suffering she made herself a circlet of a plate of silver three fingers broad, in which she fixed three rows of sharp points, thirty- three in each, in honour of the thirty-three years that the Son of God lived upon earth. Fearing that her hair, which was beginning to grow, would prevent these points from entering in, she cut it all off, excepting a handful which she left on her forehead, to hide this penitential crown from the eyes of men. She wore it underneath her veil, which made it the more painful, as these points, being unequally long, did not all pierce her head at the same time, but one after another, according to her different movements; so that with the least motion these iron thorns tore her flesh, and pierced her head in ninety-nine places with excessive pain; and as the muscles of this part are all connected with one another, our Saint could scarcely speak; and when she coughed or sneezed this violent effort caused the three rows of points to penetrate even to the skull with almost inconceivable pain.

As she had only invented this sort of torment to imitate the sufferings of the Son of God, she would have willingly changed this circlet for a crown of thorns, to imitate Him more closely; but her confessor thought it better for her not to change it, for fear that the holes which the thorns would make might suppurate. She followed his advice, seeing that it would be very difficult to conceal a crown of thorns, as the points would come through her veil, and reveal what she so much wished to hide; for this reason she made this silver crown, in which she fixed the points so firmly that after her death the goldsmith could not draw even one out with his instruments.

To increase the pain, she changed every day the place of this crown, causing new wounds, or reopening these which were beginning to heal. She had put strings at each end of this painful diadem, that by tying them closely she might force the points in more deeply; and in changing it, which she did every day, this crown caused her new pain. Every Friday, which she particularly consecrated to penance, she tied this circlet more tightly, and made it come down upon her forehead till it pierced the cartilage of her ears in many places. Her mother and the rest of the family did not perceive this crown for a long time, nor her endeavours to hide it from their view; but one day, when she was trying to save one of her brothers from the anger of her father, who was correcting him with too much violence, in pushing her away he placed his hand by chance on the sharp crown that encircled her head, and, as he was carried away by passion, his touch was so rough, that it caused three streams of blood to flow from her wounds; and this made known to her mother and all of them the great austerities which she secretly practised.

Rose, more afflicted at the discovery than at the pain of the blow, went quickly to her room, took off her crown, cleaned it, and after having washed her wounds and stopped the blood, she put on her veil as before. Her mother, having followed her, commanded her to take it off; she then saw her head pierced all round by the iron points; and though she felt as much horror as pity, she pretended not to see them, fearing that if she took from her this instrument of penance, she would only invent a more cruel one.

She did not fail to complain of it to her confessor who desired Rose to send to him, without delay, the pointed circlet which she wore round her head. She took it to him, but when he saw this crown stained with blood, and bristling with points, he was greatly surprised; and considering her delicate constitution, her age, and her frequent illnesses, he tried to persuade her to leave it off. Rose, seeing that he used remonstrance more than authority, represented to him so forcibly the necessity she felt of suffering this continual martyrdom, in order to be conformable to her Divine Spouse, that he gave it back to her, after having blunted

S. Rose Sewing, with her hermitage in the background

some of the sharpest points. This compassion did not, however, prevent her suffering the same pain as before, for the rest of the nails pierced her head when she struck the crown, or tied it with the strings. Every time that the devil tempted her, she pressed this crown three times on her head with her finger, in honour of the most holy Trinity, and this mortification made her always victorious over his attacks. After her death a great servant of God, kissing respectfully this instrument of penance, felt himself interiorly inflamed with the love of God, and was at the same time perfumed with a heavenly odour, which was a sign to him, that Almighty God had accepted this new sort of torture, which the blessed Rose had invented to mortify herself.

This faithful spouse of the Son of God had so perfectly imitated during her life-time her seraphic mistress in the pain of this thorny diadem, that after she was dead, as there were no flowers to be found to make her a crown, which is customary in Peru at the burial of young girls, as a sign of the glory they, reap from their virginity in the next world, they took, by divine inspiration, the crown of thorns from the head of a statue of S. Catherine of Siena, to place it on that of the blessed Rose: as if that seraphic lover wished to lend her crown to Rose to honour her triumph, and to conduct her in a more glorious manner to the throne of the Divinity. Several persons of known sanctity saw her enter heaven, with a palm in her hand, and a crown resplendent with light on her head, which our Blessed Lady had placed there, to acknowledge by this favour the services she had rendered her.

But let us return to the austerities and sufferings of our Saint, which merited for her the glory of this triumph. From her infancy she invented many means of making her bed hard, and her mother having perceived it, made her sleep with her; but Rose, contrived to mortify herself in her obedience, for as soon as her mother was asleep, she drew on one side the feather bed on which she had been lying, and slipped quietly on to the bedstead, placing a large stone under her head for a pillow. She practised this mortification till her mother, after telling her that this rigour was displeasing to her, and that she was obstinate, at last said she might seek a bed somewhere else, and sleep as she liked. Rose, quite delighted with this permission, made herself a bed in the form of a chest of rough wood and put in it a quantity of small stones of different sizes, that her body might suffer more, and might not enjoy the repose smooth planks would have, afforded it. This bed still seeming too soft, she put in three pieces of twisted and knotted wood, and she added seven more, filling up the spaces with three hundred pieces of broken tiles placed so as to wound her body.

This was the luxurious couch on which this insatiable lover of the cross took the rest necessary to recruit her exhausted strength. She always kept behind her pillow a bottle full of gall, with which she rubbed her eyes before going to bed, and washed her mouth in the morning, in memory of that which was given to Jesus Christ her Spouse on the cross. When Almighty God called her to this sort of crucified life, she had only a piece of coarse cloth doubled for a pillow; soon after, not finding this hard enough, she used bricks; but all this not being sufficient to satisfy her ardour for suffering, she took a rough stone for a pillow. Her mother becoming aware of it, from the bruises which this stone inflicted on her face, forbade her ever to use it again, and insisted on her having a bolster, like the rest of the family: she certainly obeyed, but in filling it with wool, as was mentioned at the commencement of this history, she put also vine branches, and bits of broken canes, in the place where she laid her head, and by this invention she rendered her pillow as hard and more painful than it was before.

She slept for fifteen years on this rough bed, if it would not be more correct to call it a cross; and it caused her such dreadful pain, that though she was very generous, and met with intrepid courage every sort of pain, still she never placed herself upon it without trembling and shuddering, and the blood seemed to freeze in her veins, so violent was the emotion which the inferior part manifested at the sight of the pain it was obliged to endure. On these occasions, when she was half dead, Jesus Christ several times appeared to her with a sweet and gracious countenance, saying to her, to rouse her courage, "Remember, my child, that the bed of the cross on which I died for the love of thee, was harder, narrower, and more painful than that on which thou art lying; think of the gall which I drank for thy sake, and call to mind the nails which pierced My Hands and Feet; thou wilt then feel consolation in the terrible pains thou sufferest on thy bed."

She was not wanting in resolution in these frightful austerities; but as this vigour did not extend to her body, she became so weak that her confessors ordered her to use more moderation, and take away at least these broken tiles, which gave her the most pain; but she begged so earnestly, that she was allowed to replace them, and to sleep upon them during the last two Lents she passed in this life. For some time before her death she passed the night in a corner of the room, where she was almost frozen with cold. The implacable hatred which she felt towards her body taught her to refuse it every comfort; for this reason she always worked standing, and when she could not continue so any longer, she made use of a very narrow piece of wood for a seat.

When near death she lost nothing of her desire to lie on a hard bed; she sought no other tortures than the excessive pain she endured thereon; and as they would not place her on the ground, as she desired, she obtained at last, by prayers and tears, that two crossed sticks should be placed under her head and shoulders, that she might expire on this cross, as Jesus Christ her Divine Spouse

had died upon His. Some persons of piety who saw her die, perceived on her countenance that of the Son of God, with the same appearance as He had when dying on Calvary. Blessed Raymond of Capua had formerly observed the same in visiting S. Catherine of Siena when she was ill.

The insupportable hardness of her bed shows that she watched most part of the night, as it prevented her from sleeping. She confined herself to two hours sleep, and often did not spend the whole of them in sleep; she so disposed of the remaining time, that she passed twelve hours in a perpetual application of her mind to God by prayer, and the others she spent in needlework or other employments, to relieve the poverty of her parents.

Though her fasts, her hair shirt, the hardness of her bed, her almost continual meditations, and other austerities, had given her a great facility in watching, the devil did not fail to use many artifices to induce her to sleep; but she knew how to detect them, and to overcome his efforts she struck her head roughly against the wall, gave herself hard blows, and sometimes she fixed her hands to the arms of a large cross which was in her room, and thus her body hung suspended in the air; and if in spite of all these efforts she still felt overcome with sleep, she fastened the small quantity of hair, she had left on her head to hide her crown of thorns, to a large nail fixed in the wall, and thus she triumphed over the temptation.

"And thus she overcame the temptation."

CHAPTER VII

OF HER SOLITUDE, AND THE HERMITAGE WHICH SHE HAD BUILT IN HER FATHER'S GARDEN, THAT SHE MIGHT LIVE QUITE SEPARATED FROM MEN.

Solitude is a sort of Paradise to souls that aspire to virtue, either because being there solely occupied with the perfections of God, they are raised above the condition of mortals and become quite divine, or on account of the graces which Almighty God then pours out upon them more abundantly, and the familiarity with Himself to which He raises them. As His Spirit is incompatible with that of the world, He is pleased with solitude, and He seems to reserve His caresses for these who separate themselves from the world to enjoy the sweetness of His conversation. Thus, speaking of a soul who wishes to keep a close union, with Him, He says that He will draw her into solitude, where being disengaged, from creatures He will speak to her heart, that is, He will converse familiarly with her, to show her the path she must follow to attain heaven.

The blessed Rose, while yet a child, felt herself so forcibly drawn to solitude, that she sought the most secret corners of the house, and deprived herself of all these little amusements with which children of her age usually divert themselves, that she might attend solely to God, and not to interrupt the incredible pleasure she began to feel in her sweet

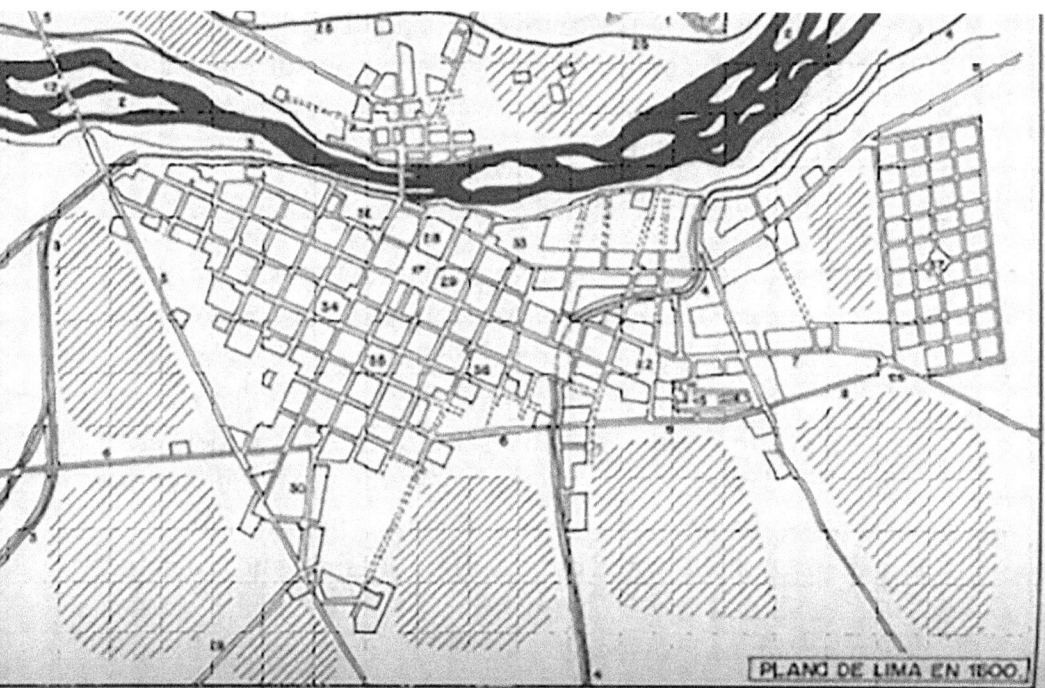
PLANO DE LIMA EN 1600

communications with Him. This desire of being hidden from the eyes of men, in order to converse more familiarly with her beloved Spouse, increasing with her age, she made a little hut in her father's garden, with palm leaves, and other branches of trees, and she wove them so carefully, that the sun had great difficulty in penetrating. She remained there nearly all day; so that it was generally said in the house, "If you wish to find Rose, you must look for her in the garden; that is her bedroom, her table, and her oratory; she never leaves it." When she was older, she could not suffer a greater torment than to be drawn from her retreat to converse with creatures. She did all she could, by prayers and tears, to prevail upon her mother to allow her some part of the house, where she would not be seen, and no longer to oblige her to go with her to the town. Though her mother did indulge her in some degree, she still required her, in spite of her repugnance, to go with her sometimes to pay her visits. One day, when she had been ordered to dress smartly on this account, she pulled out of the oven as she passed a large stone, which fell so heavily on her foot, that she was obliged to remain at home, for the wound, of which she had been herself the cause, made her walk lame, and gave her great pain.

One reason which contributed greatly to give her an aversion for company was, that the fame of her sanctity being spread over the whole town, she was spoken of in her presence as a person of great sanctity and close union with God: and these praises gave her the more pain, as she was fully persuaded of her misery and unworthiness. This made her resolve to choose another state of life, to be delivered from this slavery, and to be no longer obliged to follow the fashions and maxims of the world. Foreseeing the difficulties which her mother would oppose to this design, and believing that she should never obtain her consent without a special interposition of Providence, she had recourse to the Blessed Virgin, her ordinary refuge in her necessities; and earnestly entreated her to dispose the mind of her mother to consent to her desire of embracing a more retired life, and to allow her to make profession of a life of devotion, that she might be dispensed from the customs of the world, which she could not endure. In order to obtain this favour, which she so passionately desired, she begged the father sacristan to put on the neck of the statue of our Lady of the Rosary, a chaplet of coral which she kept in her box, assuring him that he would do her a great kindness, as it was of great consequence to her to gain the favour of the Blessed Virgin, that the Divine Infant whom she held in her arms might become her security for a grace which she fervently solicited from Him. Though these words were an enigma to the good father, he promised to present her rosary; but as the ladder was not there, he thought no more about it, till Rose, noticing his omission, repeated her petition; he then immediately sent for a ladder, and in presence of these who were in the chapel, he put the rosary on the image of the Blessed Virgin.

Some days after, the chaplet was seen in the divine hands of the Infant Jesus, as if it had been taken from the Mother, expressly to give it to the Son. This prodigy very much surprised those who frequented the church, particularly the father sacristan, who declared that no one had made the exchange, and that it must have been an effect of the power of Almighty God. Rose herself interpreted it in her favour, and saw it with great delight, knowing by this sign that our Blessed Lady had obtained the favour she had asked, and that Jesus Christ her Divine Son held this rosary, in order to answer for His blessed Mother, and to show her that He had taken upon Himself the execution of her pious design.

With this confidence she requested her mother, through the Rev. Father John of Laurenzana, Don Gonzalez and his wife, Mary of Usategni, to allow her a little room apart, into which no one of the family, or from out of doors, might enter to speak to her or visit her, except her confessor, to whom she was obliged to give an account of her proceedings from time to time. Her mother, who till then had been inflexible to her tears and entreaties, gave her leave to do as she pleased, in consideration of those who made the request. This consent being obtained, she had a little hermitage built in the garden, five feet long and four wide. One of her confessors found it too narrow, but she answered pleasantly, that it was large enough for her, and for Jesus Christ, her adorable Spouse.

Some days after she had shut herself up there, a holy woman, who had frequent ecstasies, saw in a rapture the blessed Rose like a brilliant star, the rays of which not being confined to the limits of this small cell, pierced through the walls on every side, to spread themselves over the town of Lima. She remained buried in this hermitage as a person dead to the world, always occupied either in prayer or penance, or in some work, and so absorbed in God, that living more to Him than to herself, she did not know whether her soul were separated from her body, or still animated it in its operations.

The fame of her virtue induced the first ladies of the town to visit her, to enjoy the sweetness of her conversation, and to profit by her example. As she could not forbid them the house, and as they were careful to request her mother's assistance, who enabled them to see her, and who took them to her retreat, Rose received them, though against her will, deploring the time she thought she lost in these civilities; and though they only spoke of Almighty God, our Saint said that it was much more agreeable and profitable to her to speak with God, than to speak of God.

This retired life made her much talked about, especially when she was not seen to come so often to church as before; for this is customary with devout persons, whose good example inspires piety, and often attracts to God persons who are much engaged with the world by their business or rank in life. One person being scandalized at this excessive solitude, asked her why she no longer went to mass every day; Rose answered, that not being able to leave the house without her mother, who was detained at home by the cares of her household, Jesus Christ supplied for it in a miraculous manner, favouring her so far, that while she still remained in her hermitage, she heard every mass that was said in the hospital of the Holy Ghost, and even those celebrated in the church of S. Augustine, which was four or five streets distant from her house. In fact, it was remarked several times, that our Saint had this gift from God, of assisting in spirit at all the sermons that were preached in the churches of Lima, and of giving as exact an account of them as if she had been actually present.

Her body being so obedient to the laws of her mind, and her mind so perfectly submissive to the will of God, we need not be surprised that irrational animals should have respected her virtue, and given her proofs of their obedience. The dampness of the earth, and the foliage of the trees which surrounded the hermitage of this happy solitary, drew thither an almost innumerable quantity of mosquitoes, which abound in America; and although these little insects love the shade, and always seek it, particularly at noon, when the heat of the sun is almost insupportable, and at night to be sheltered from the cold; still, not one of this legion of flies, which covered the walls, the windows, and the doors of her cell, presumed to settle upon her; they showed so much respect for her person that they seemed to honour in her the sovereign power of God, who had created them. They did not show the same deference to her mother, nor to the persons who came to see her in her retreat by the permission of her spiritual guides, for they were severely stung.

Three years before her death, she retired to the house of Don Gonzalez de la Massa, in obedience to her parents, who were anxious to allow him this favour, which he had earnestly solicited; and here she caused to be built for her a room as small as that which she had occupied at home, in which she passed her whole time, both day and night, in prayer, except when she returned, as she did from time to time, to her first hermitage, to avoid the intercourse of creatures, and to enjoy the company of Almighty God in that solitude

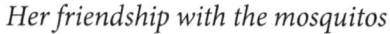

Her friendship with the mosquitos

The Espousal

CHAPTER VIII

JESUS CHRIST ESPOUSES THE BLESSED ROSE, IN THE PRESENCE OF THE EVER BLESSED VIRGIN.

Love always tends to union, and the greater the love the closer is the alliance to which it aspires; and as there is not a closer union than that which joins a man and woman in marriage, Almighty God makes use of this expression to assist us to comprehend the union which He contracts with just souls by grace and charity. Thus He assures the faithful soul that He will espouse her; that is, that He will raise her to the honour of an alliance with Him, and will give her a share in His Heart, and in His caresses. It is true that sanctifying grace procures this advantage for all the just in an invisible and hidden manner; but as there are souls singularly favoured and caressed by God, and with whom He is more closely connected, He sometimes also espouses them in a visible manner, with a ceremonial of pomp and magnificence. The blessed Rose had read in the life of S. Catherine of Siena, her dear mistress, that Jesus Christ had raised this seraphic lover to so great a degree of glory and favour, that He espoused her solemnly in the presence of the Blessed Virgin, S. Dominic, and several other Saints. Though the love she bore to the same Divine Saviour made her sigh after the enjoyment of a similar grace, the consciousness of her own misery and nothingness kept her in such profound humility, that she would have thought it a crime to harbour the thought, or to form a single desire of it; and this very humility, which made her judge herself unworthy of it, was the precious portion which captivated the Heart of the Son of God, and induced Him to honour her in a similar manner.

He disposed her for this divine alliance by miracles; for the mysterious black

"He showed her an almost innumerable company of virgins...."

and white butterfly, of which we have already spoken, after having long fluttered on the left side of her, at last settled exactly over her heart, and did not move till it had traced the resemblance of a heart on the dress of our Saint. At this moment she seemed to hear an interior voice saying to her with great sweetness, "Rose, My beloved, give Me thy heart," as if Jesus Christ wished her to understand by this enigmatic representation, that He would give her His Heart in exchange for hers, and renew in her person the miracle He had formerly performed in favour of S. Catherine of Siena, when He took away her heart, in order to put His own in its place.

One night when the blessed Rose was absorbed in contemplation, Jesus Christ appeared to her as a most beautiful man, and told her with a smiling countenance, that she was an object of His love; and after this delightful assurance, He showed her an almost innumerable troop of virgins resplendent with brightness, who were occupied in sawing and cutting marble, and He invited her to join the number of these chaste spouses, whom she saw employed in this hard labour. She began to consider in her mind this scene, which ravished her with admiration, and at the same instant she saw herself covered with a mantle woven of gold and precious stones, and she was placed in the company of these happy virgins.

It is painful to make known to carnal men, who comprehend not the wonders of God, and who are scandalized at the ineffable condescension which He shows to souls inflamed with His love, the present with which He honoured the blessed Rose, to invite her to the dignity of being His spouse. On Palm Sunday, a day on which the Church celebrates the solemn and triumphant entrance of the Son of God into the city of Jerusalem, amidst the acclamations of the people, the sacristan, who distributed palms to the other sisters of her order, who were in the church, passed her without giving her one, either through inadvertence, or by the special permission of God. Rose thought this must have happened through her fault, and that she must have been distracted during the distribution. Afflicted and confounded, she retired into the chapel of our Lady of the Rosary, where, placing herself on her knees, she began to sigh and weep, to expiate her fault.

While she was soliciting by her tears the pardon of the negligence she thought she had committed, she saw that the Blessed Virgin had a smiling countenance; and that after having looked upon her graciously, she turned to speak to her Son, and, as if she had received from Him a favourable answer to her request, she turned her eyes again towards the blessed Rose, as if to congratulate her on the happiness to which she was going to be raised. Our Saint, transported with a secret joy, which she did not usually feel, raised her eyes to look at the Son of God, who, looking at her again, caused a torrent of delight to flow into the soul of this chaste lover, and said to

S. Vincent Ferrer, S. Rose and S. Louis Beltran

her these tender and loving words : "Rose of My Heart, I take thee for My spouse."

Quite enraptured with the honour of this illustrious alliance, she prostrated herself humbly at the feet of Jesus Christ, and entering into the abyss of her miseries, she said to Him with profound respect, " Lord, behold Thy handmaid; I am too much honoured by the quality of Thy slave, and I bear in my soul the indelible marks of a necessary slavery, which render me unworthy of the glorious rank of Thy spouse."

The consideration of her own nothingness would have made her take this heavenly favour for an illusion, had not the Blessed Virgin assured her of the truth of this mystery by these gracious words, "Rose, the beloved of my Son, see to what an excess of glory He has raised thee; by His mercy thou art now truly His spouse." As her humility, however, made her still apprehend some delusion in this grace, of which she judged herself very unworthy, Jesus Christ, to give her confidence, graciously confirmed to her the truth of the alliance He had contracted with her in the presence of His holy Mother. Who could express the supernatural gifts of grace which she received from her Divine Spouse in consequence of this august union? We can only know what she herself made known to a learned man who directed her. When he urged her one day to declare to him what gift her Heavenly Spouse had bestowed on her as the pledge of His love and their alliance, she confessed that she was not possessed of eloquence sufficient to express the magnificent liberality which God had exercised in her regard without considering her unworthiness.

That she might always have a sensible mark of this illustrious alliance before her eyes, she begged her brother to have a ring made for her; he took the measure for it, and though he knew nothing of this mystery, he told his sister that he would have engraved upon it, "Rose of My Heart, I take thee for My spouse." This consoled her very much for she saw that Almighty God had inspired him to choose these words.

On Maundy Thursday she begged the sacristan to put this precious pledge of the love of Jesus Christ into that part of the tabernacle in which the most Adorable Sacrament is enclosed; but on Easter Sunday she was much surprised to see this ring on her finger, though she had not asked for it back, and the religious whom she had asked to enclose it had not returned it to her. She knew at once by this miracle that her Divine Spouse had communicated to this metal the property of returning to her finger, only to show her His ardent desire of being intimately united to her heart; and that as He had become everything to her by this alliance, she should make Him the sole object of her thoughts and affections. This miracle was very evident; for her mother, who was beside her in the church, and who closely watched her, saw this ring on her finger without having seen anyone approach to place it there.

A year after our Saint's death, a great servant of God, holding this ring in his hand, was sweetly ravished into an ecstasy; and among other ineffable consolations which Almighty God poured abundantly into his soul, he perceived this faithful spouse of Jesus Christ very high in glory, and honourably placed among the greatest saints in heaven. Quite enraptured with joy at this delightful spectacle, he wished to extend his hand to retain it, but he was not able: the ring seemed to have benumbed his arm. If this nuptial ring worked so great a wonder on this servant of God, who can conceive the power with which it acted on the soul of this chaste spouse?

CHAPTER IX

OF THE CLOSE UNION WITH GOD TO WHICH SHE ATTAINED BY MEANS OF MENTAL PRAYER.

The Holy Spirit having chosen the blessed Rose as His temple, became Himself her Master, and taught her from her earliest infancy how to pray. The supernatural lights with which He enriched her understanding inflamed her heart with so ardent a love for this holy exercise, that even sleep itself, which by the necessity of nature she was compelled to take, could not distract her from it; for her imagination was so completely absorbed in it, that she was often heard to repeat while asleep the same number of vocal prayers as she had said during the day. Her piety increasing with her years, she applied herself wholly to God from her twelfth year by the prayer of union, by means of which "the soul becomes one spirit with Him," according to the words of S. Paul. She had two different methods of conversing with God, one in solitude, when, having disengaged her mind from the care of earthly things, she retired to her hermitage, or to some other place apart from creatures, to attend solely and uninterruptedly to God; the other, in any place or in any employment that occupied her, for she kept her mind so united to God, and recollected in Him, that she prayed in working or in exercising charity towards the afflicted: thus, whether she walked, worked, or whatever she did, she was always in prayer.

She employed every day twelve hours in the first kind of prayer, as we have already mentioned; the second was continual, unless she was interrupted by the representations of horrible phantoms, of which we shall speak in the next chapter; so that she prayed without interruption, according to the advice of the great Apostle, for whether she slept or watched, whether she conversed, ate, read spiritual books, went abroad, or remained in her cell, God was incessantly in her thoughts, and she entertained herself with Him in loving colloquies. It is beyond the power of our imagination to conceive how, though the presence of God entirely engrossed all the interior powers of her soul, she still acted in exterior things with great presence of mind, giving the proper answers to questions, and finishing the work she commenced. Even if she were engaged in household employments, the cares which would have much embarrassed another, did not divert her from the presence of her Spouse, nor from the continual conversation she kept up with Him in her heart, in which He communicated to her His choicest favours.

In the time of prayer her senses were so recollected, that they represented nothing to her imagination which could distract her from her intercourse with God; when in the church she fixed her eyes steadfastly on the altar, and never looked at anything else; she was so absorbed in attention to the Divine mysteries, that she never knew who passed before her; and it was often remarked, that on certain occasions which inspired others with fear or surprise, she did not move a muscle, remaining motionless as a rock, while others in the church were quite terrified. After having passed hours, the whole day, and even all the night in prayer, she was often found in the position in which she had first placed herself. Towards the end of her life she remained in prayer in her hermitage from Maundy Thursday till Easter Sunday, her mind being so united to God, and so completely disengage from the senses, that her body lost all strength, and she could neither rise nor support herself.

She meditated every day three hours on the benefits of God, and the innumerable graces she had received from His mercy. She had for some time applied herself to a very sublime kind of prayer, which was, to meditate on a hundred and fifty perfections of God; after having drawn from it many holy affections which enkindled in her heart the flames of Divine love, she honoured each of these attributes separately, with an adoration of *latria*. Her mind was agitated with many different sensations during this prayer, as it formed affections conformable to the effects which we attribute to the sovereign perfections of God; fear, hope, grief, confusion, joy, desires, and compassion, had a share in her sentiments, when she contemplated His justice, His mercy, His omnipotence, His wisdom, and the other attributes which occupied her thoughts; and she felt two different sorts of agitation, similar to the two contrary pulsations which physicians recognize in our hearts, which succeed one another; now the consideration of the avenging justice of God plunged her into the depths; soon after, a reflection on His mercy elevated her to heaven.

This method of prayer was not only very agreeable to God, but our Saint testified that it was also terrible to the devils. Her love of God, which continually increased by the consideration of His Divine attributes, made her words like burning coals, which lighted up the same fire in the hearts of these with whom she conversed; for she was careful to make use of everything to lead them to love virtue and hate vice. If she walked with them in a garden, she spoke to them of the sovereign beauty of God, which spreads itself over flowers as a mirror, in which men may see the faint representation of that Source of beauty from which they derive their colour and brightness.

She made use of this means with no less advantage herself to raise her heart to God, adoring Him in all sublunary things, which she considered as animated pictures, representing to her His excellences and perfections. It usually happened that everything she saw or heard elevated her mind above her senses, even so as to throw her into a rapture. One day when she was ill, and something was being prepared for her to eat, a little bird came and perched near the window of her room, and began to sing,; where upon our Saint applied herself so earnestly to the consideration of the goodness of God, Who had given this bird so sweet a note to sing His praises, that she was ravished into an ecstasy, in which she continued transported with love, from nine in the morning till evening.

The year of her death, another bird, whose melody was most charming, placed itself opposite her room during the whole of Lent; as soon as the sun began to go down the blessed Rose ordered him to employ his notes in praising God; he obeyed, and raising his voice sang with all his strength, till this spouse of Christ, unwilling to be outdone by a bird in offering to God canticles of praise and benediction, which was more her duty than his, began to sing hymns to His glory, which she did very sweetly; when she had finished this little chorister began again, and thus together they composed a choir in which they sang alternately for an hour the praises of God. At six o'clock she dismissed him till the next day, and he was so punctual that he never failed to appear at the time fixed.

The abundant graces which she received from God in mental prayer made her exhort every one to embrace the practice of it. She spent several hours every day in reading books which taught the method of meditation, and in particular the works of Father Lewis of Granada.

She had wonderful eloquence in persuading others to it; she begged confessors to exhort their penitents, and preachers to speak of the excellence of meditation, and of its necessity

for all who wish to lead a holy life corresponding with their dignity as Christians, and with the obligation of saving their souls. Since the Rosary of the Blessed Virgin comprises both mental and vocal prayer, in the words and mysteries which compose it, she wished all who mounted the pulpit to instruct the people, and exhort them to embrace this devotion and to say at least a part of it every day. Her zeal and example induced many persons to practise it.

She collects water from a fountain

CHAPTER X

SHE IS TORMENTED WITH INTERIOR PAINS, TO SO FRIGHTFUL A DEGREE, THAT SHE IS EXAMINED BY SOME DIVINES, WHO DECLARE HER STATE TO BE FROM GOD.

The life of this Saint verifies perfectly that oracle of the Holy Ghost, that God tries those souls whom He predestines to glory, and that the greatest favours He lavishes upon them in this life, are the preludes to these interior crosses which He prepares in order to purify them.

The blessed Rose having attained to a very close and perpetual union with God, began to be attacked every day at certain intervals with such frightful darkness and obscurity, that she was often a whole hour without being able to distinguish whether she were in hell with the condemned, or in purgatory with the souls who there satisfy the justice of God. In this horrible darkness she had no thought of God, no idea of His mercies; and to fill up her chalice of bitterness, she had in her mind a confused remembrance of the love she had had for Him. As under this desolation she found herself in a very different condition from her former happy state, she imagined that she no longer knew God, and that she was reduced to the dreadful state of never being able to love Him. While these clouds of darkness obscured her mind, she thought she considered Almighty God as a stranger, an unknown person, in a word, as something as far from her thoughts and ideas, as if she had never had any union or friendship with Him.

In this species of desolation she seemed to see before her eyes an impassable wall which hindered her from escaping from this labyrinth, which made her believe that her condition differed in nothing from the pain of loss which the damned suffer in the privation of the beatific vision. As death is the termination of misfortunes to the miserable, she tried to soften the rigour of the terrible pains she suffered by the hope of dying soon; but instantly reflecting that her soul was immortal, and that death, which is so great a relief to others, would not be the end of her sorrows, this thought raised fears which would have been capable of throwing her into despair, if that same Providence of God which permitted these desolations, had not preserved her from it.

This darkness and trouble of mind tormented her for fifteen years, at least a hour and a half every day; her efforts to banish them from her mind, only made them more importunate; and this afflicted Rose found sharp thorns within herself, which lacerated her soul, from the belief she felt that she was abandoned by God.

In fine, the evil spirits filled her imagination with frightful spectres, and troubled her mind by such fearful visions, that though this courageous virgin could calmly bear the most insupportable pain, still she never could accustom herself to this sort of trial, the bare thought of which was so terrible to her, that when she felt the hour of her sufferings drawing near, she threw herself on the ground, at the feet of Jesus Christ, and, bathed in tears, she earnestly besought Him not to oblige her to drink this chalice of horror and bitterness, offering herself to the most cruel sort of death, which she would infinitely prefer, to the ceasing to love Him one moment; because God, being to her what the soul is to the body, she thought herself deprived every day of that supernatural and divine life during these storms: knowing, however, that it was by the will of God she suffered these pains, she adored it with respect, and said to Him, with a mind resigned to the orders of His Providence, "Lord, may Thy will be done, not mine; I abandon myself to Thy Divine dispensations." These anxieties, this darkness, and this species of desolation, exercised the judgment of the most famous theologians of Lima, and there were very few who gave a decided opinion; some believed that she was deluded, or that what passed in her mind was the effect of her long watchings; others, that they were illusions of the devil, which disturbed her imagination; others again attributed them to the heavy vapours which her great abstinence caused to mount from her stomach to her brain.

She listened to them humbly, and modestly said, that the little knowledge they had of her state was the effect of her stupidity, which could not explain how these things passed in her interior. She did not fail to attempt sometimes, in order to obey them, to give them some idea of her pains by comparisons; but when she had compared them to fire, which seemed most properly to express their violence, she frankly confessed that there was no relation between what she suffered in her soul, and the pain which the activity of that element causes.

When she spoke of her desolations, she said that she seemed to see herself very remote from God by a great dissimilarity, that she felt overcome by her timidity, and in these sorrowful moments she imagined herself overwhelmed by the tempest, of which the royal prophet speaks, which these sad thoughts raised in her soul; she added, that during this darkness, she wished to become anathema, that is, separated from Jesus Christ her God and her Spouse; she said, in fine, that these representations afflicted her to that degree, that they would have each day caused her death, if God had not preserved her life by a continual miracle. She was not the only soul whom Almighty God has tried in this terrible manner: we read the same thing of S. Catherine of Siena; and the history of the blessed Henry Suso, religious of the Order of Friars Preachers, relates that the Son of God often appeared to him under the form of a judge, with an inflamed countenance, and eyes sparkling with anger, pronouncing with a voice of thunder these overwhelming words: " Go, ye cursed, into everlasting fire."

Being asked if after being thus separated from God, and suffering this eclipse of the Divine Sun in her soul, she did not receive from Him some consolation; she answered, that God entered again into her mind with so brilliant a light, and enkindled so great a love in her will, that it became inflamed with ardour; after which she re-entered the Bosom of God, and was therein so perfectly transformed into her Beloved, that she seemed to be closely united with Him, and so confirmed in His grace, that not all the temptations of the flesh, the devils, or men, could ever separate her from His love.

Though God had revealed to her, and had clearly shown her that she was in the sure way of salvation and perfection; still, as she was very humble, she never refused to appear before these who wished to examine her vocation and manner of life. Besides her confessor, who studied her for a long time, many persons celebrated for their learning and piety, as well of the Order of Friars Preachers, as of the Society of Jesus, and even the famous Doctor John of Castile, a man very well versed in the mystical life, and who composed an excellent treatise upon it, carefully examined all that passed in her interior. After having conferred together several times on her life, and the extraordinary things which happened to her, they remarked, First, that from her infancy she experienced ardent desires of loving God alone, and so powerful an attraction to prayer, that she found nothing sweeter than to entertain herself with God by prayer, and to raise her mind incessantly to the contemplation of heavenly things. Secondly, that till the age of twelve years she had pursued different methods in prayer, which had all raised her to a high degree of spirituality. Thirdly, that her whole life was a continual exercise of patience under the crosses she had suffered in every way, and from the delicacy of her body, her abstinence, her want of sleep, and her sicknesses. Fourthly, that she had attained so perfect a union with God, that she could not turn her thoughts from Him, even if she had wished to apply them to something else; hence, she was never diverted from Him by her exterior occupations, nor by the violence of her illnesses, which caused her excessive pain. They remarked that Almighty God was so present to her, in all the faculties of her soul, and excited in her so sweet a hope of being favoured with His graces, that it was quite impossible for her to find any pleasure on earth, except in the continual idea she had of His mercies.

Being asked if she had ever read books treating of mystical theology; she answered humbly, that she was not aware that

S. Rose with her inquisitors

there were any bearing this title, or which taught the method of prayer, which conducts to the unitive life. When she was asked what efforts she had made to resist her evil inclinations, she answered, that, by the grace of God, she did not remember to have ever found any opposition in her soul to virtue; that on the contrary, she had felt from her infancy a strong inclination to piety, which had made her joyously embrace its practice. "1 do not mean" she said, "that I have not perceived in myself involuntary movements, but as soon as I applied my mind to the presence of God, they vanished so promptly that I had not usually time to resist them." They wished further to know if she did not find some trifling satisfaction in earthly things, when her mind became a little relaxed from its violent application to God in prayer; she said, that she could not possibly take the least pleasure in them, and that she suffered inconceivable pain when her mind was a moment unoccupied with God.

These divines, after several conferences, concluded that her life was the work of God; that she suffered in some degree the torments which the souls in purgatory endure by these representations, which oppressed her with fear, and threw her into a sort of agony; and that God permitted by a dispensation of His Providence that she should be tormented with these apprehensions of hell, and that her understanding should be obscured by this darkness, in order to keep her humble, and to purify her love more and more.

These holy men having commanded her, in virtue of obedience, to explain to them the state in which she was after this dryness and terrible desolation, she blushed at this order; she showed evidently by the colour that rose to her face the pain she felt in declaring secrets which had God alone for witness; she obeyed, but with so much confusion that her voice faltered as she declared, that after this storm Jesus Christ appeared visibly to her, now as a Child, again as of thirty years of age; that the Blessed Virgin came usually to console her with so amiable a countenance that her looks brought consolation to her soul.

She added, that these frequent visions worked in her three good effects. First, an abundance of joy, which made her insensible to all the pleasures of the world. Secondly, a love and an attachment to God, which separated her entirely from creatures. Thirdly, so admirable a tranquillity of the passions, that she knew nothing on earth capable of disturbing her peace; whence they conjectured that she was in a sure way of great perfection. Some other theologians, from the account they had heard of the profound manner in which she spoke of the inscrutable mystery of the Trinity of the Divine Persons, of the hypostatical union of the Word with the Human Nature, of the Book of Life, predestination, nature, and grace, and other mysteries of faith, had the curiosity to converse with her on these sublime subjects. After a long conference with her, they confessed that they had never known a more enlightened soul, and that our Saint had not attained the knowledge of these mysteries by the vivacity of her mind, nor by her application to study; but that God had given her the understanding of them, by an infused knowledge, and that she was only the organ of the Holy Ghost when she spoke of these elevated truths of religion.

One thing which surprised the most experienced in the mystical life was, that she had attained the unitive life with very little exercise of the laborious practices of the purgative; and they remarked with astonishment a sort of combat between God and her, without being able to determine whether God was more occupied in seeking in the secrets of His wisdom the means of exercising her by suffering, than she was disposed to suffer them for His love; for she showed an incredible avidity for crosses, and an invincible patience which rendered her victorious over her trials, and over every affliction which Almighty God sent to exercise her love and fidelity. Hence the most learned and the greatest masters of the spiritual life who had assembled to examine her, made known publicly that she was governed by the Spirit of God, and that she acted by the impulse of grace in her conduct.

Louisa of Melgarcyo, a lady of known sanctity, was so persuaded of this, that every time she met the blessed Rose she threw herself on her knees before her, notwithstanding the resistance her modesty made to prevent her; and when our Saint had passed on, this virtuous woman noticed where her feet had trod in walking, and kissed the traces with respect and veneration.

CHAPTER XI

OF THE FAMILIAR MANNER IN WHICH JESUS CHRIST, THE BLESSED VIRGIN, S. CATHERINE OF SIENA, AND HER GUARDIAN ANGEL CONVERSED WITH HER; AND OF THE VICTORIES WHICH SHE GAINED OVER THE DEVILS WHO TEMPTED HER.

If we separate love from familiarity, we deprive it of its delight and sweetness: and when Aristotle judged that there could be no friendship between God and men, it was because he considered the familiar communications which are inseparable from it derogatory to the profound respect which they owe to the Divinity, and dangerous on account of the liberty which they might allow themselves, and which would be capable of drawing down His hatred and aversion; and because this philosopher never knew the tenderness of God towards men, nor the mystery of the Incarnation, by which He has made Himself like them. The Christian religion, more enlightened in, its sentiments, recognizes a perfect friendship between God and the just man, by grace, and believes that God does not only honour by familiarity these souls who love Him tenderly, but that He bestows on them favours, which we may call a delicious foretaste of the happiness prepared for them in Heaven. The lives of the Saints are full of examples of this, and that of our Saint furnishes us with authentic proofs of it.

The Son of God not only appeared visibly to the blessed Rose at the time when her trials left her, He frequently visited her when she was reading her spiritual books, working, or embroidering, under the form of a beautiful Infant, stretching out Its little arms to caress her, and to testify the excess of Its love. Rose was so accustomed to these visions, that when her Divine Spouse was one moment later than usual in appearing, she made tender complaints to Him; and as love inspires the soul with poetry, she composed elegies, to express the pain His delay caused her.

Being once indisposed with a very bad sore throat Jesus Christ visited her more frequently than usual, and treated her with inconceivable marks of goodness; and as our Saint thought she could not have a more favourable opportunity for soliciting relief from her continual suffering, He granted what she asked, on condition that He should ask something of her. Rose having agreed, and promised to execute faithfully whatever obedience should require from her, He told her that He wished her to return to her former state of suffering: she consented, provided He would increase her pains, which was the condition of her promise. When she was one day relating these favours with great innocence and candour to her mother, to console her grief in seeing her always ill, the mother saw rays dart from the face of her daughter, which so heightened her beauty, that she seemed to her an angel from Heaven, and no longer a creature subject to so many infirmities.

One night, when she was taking her rest in the oratory, which was built in the garden, a great faintness came over her; and feeling a great want of some cordial drink to strengthen her, Jesus Christ applied the Wound of His sacred side to her mouth, and this chaste lover imbibed from it a delicious nectar, as S. Catherine of Siena had formerly done; so that after receiving this extraordinary favour, S. Rose was no longer merely the spiritual daughter of this seraphic lover; she became her foster-sister having drunk from the same source from which she derived her ardour and love.

Being at the house of a lady of quality, after a long

conversation on heavenly things, Rose left the lady to go and say her prayers: during her prayer a little girl of seven years old saw the Infant Jesus with her, in a human form, dressed in a variously coloured garment, caressing her in a thousand ways, which this child related. In the house of the Lady Isabel Mexia, the Infant Jesus was seen walking familiarly with our Saint, speaking to her, and following her everywhere. Those who witnessed these innocent familiarities, saw a dazzling light stream from the pavement on which the blessed Rose walked during their conversation. As this incomparable Spouse gave Himself wholly to her, He wished to be the sole possessor of her heart and its affections; and one day He made known to her that He was jealous of a flower which she was fond of. When she was walking one day in her garden, in which she cultivated very beautiful flowers, she saw that a quantity had been gathered; not knowing who had done her this injury, she complained of it to her Spouse, but was much surprised that instead of consoling her, He made her this loving reproof: " Why art thou attached to flowers, which the sun causes to fade? Am I not the Flower of the fields, infinitely more precious than all these which thou raisest in thy garden with so much care? Thou art a flower, and thou lovest flowers! O Rose, give Me thy love; know that it is I who pulled them, that thou mayest no longer give any creature a share in that heart which belongs to Me."

The Blessed Virgin frequently honoured her with the same caresses and familiarity. This is very evident when we mention that this Queen of Angels took upon herself the care of awaking her. The continual application of her mind to God, and her extraordinary austerities, had so heated her blood, that she had almost lost the use of sleep. Her confessors desired her for some time to use every day, lettuce, endive, and poppy seeds, in order to recover it; but as these remedies only procured a very small portion of necessary repose, she found herself so overcome with drowsiness at her usual hour of rising, that she had the greatest difficulty in waking. In this necessity she had recourse to the Blessed Virgin, whom the Church calls the "Morning Star," and earnestly entreated her to have the goodness to wake her at the appointed hour. Our Lady had the goodness to grant her this favour; she appeared to her every morning, and, after awaking her, she animated her to rise by these tender words: "Rose, my child, arise; it is time to prepare yourself for prayer." She was once so overcome with drowsiness, that she fell asleep after having been awakened. The Blessed Virgin came again, and touching her gently, said, "Arise, Rose, and do not be slothful." When the Blessed Virgin had given her this little reproof, she went away differently from her usual manner of retiring, for she always allowed Rose to see her face till she had left the room, and this time she turned her back towards her, in punishment of her idleness.

From the time that Almighty God appointed S. Catherine of Siena to be her mistress, Rose had such frequent conversations with her, that the features of this seraphic virgin seemed to have been transferred to her countenance, as it happened to Moses, who was completely transformed by God after he had spoken with Him on the mountain; for she resembled her so perfectly, that she passed in the opinion of all for a second S. Catherine of Siena.

She lived also in most familiar intercourse with her guardian angel; for when Jesus Christ, her dear Spouse, was a moment later than usual in visiting her at the ordinary time, she sent her guardian angel to seek Him.

She felt one night when in her hermitage the threatenings of a fainting fit, or some similar attack, and immediately returned to the house, for fear of being taken ill in that retired place, where no one could help her. Her mother, seeing her much changed, and with the perspiration on her forehead, thought she was going to die; she told the servant to run to the nearest confectioner's to buy some chocolate, which at

Lima is commonly composed of cocoa, lemons, and sugar, to strengthen her; but our Saint begged her mother not to buy it, assuring her that she should not have long to wait for it. Her mother grew angry, and told the servant a second time to go immediately to the place she had named. Rose, seeing her eagerness, told her to call her back, and not to trouble herself, for some would be brought to her immediately from the house of the Receiver. Scarcely had she finished speaking when a servant entered the house, and brought her a large silver cup full of chocolate from his master. Her mother, greatly surprised at so seasonable an assistance, ordered her, in virtue of her authority, to tell her how she knew that this remedy would be brought to her. Rose smiled, and confessed that as her good angel always did what she asked him, she had sent him to the Receiver's wife, to tell her of her illness, and of her want of a little chocolate to restore her strength.

Her mother opened the garden gate every night before she went to bed, that her daughter might go to her room when she returned at midnight from her hermitage. She forgot it once; and when Rose was preparing to return she saw from the window a white shadow fluttering, and apparently inviting her to follow it. She thought at once that it was her guardian angel concealed under this form: she followed, and when they arrived together at the closed door, it opened of itself the instant the shadow touched it.

She was not only familiar with the holy angel that Almighty God had appointed as her own protector, but with these of others also, as she made known to one of her friends, a religious, who having a long journey to take, came to recommend himself to her good prayers. He was fortunate at first; but when he had reached the vast plains of Truxillo, which is a fine town near the sea, he underwent great fatigue, and was twice in danger of losing his life. On his return to Lima he complained to the blessed Rose, that she had not helped him in his perils, as he had asked her before he left.

She answered, that these misfortunes happened by his own fault, as he was not then in the same state as when he came to say farewell to her. She then charitably mentioned to him some things which she could only have known through his guardian angel

If the angels loved and respected her, the devils, on the other hand, had so great an aversion for her, that there was nothing they did not attempt in order to make her feel the effects of their hatred and fury. The devil attacked her once in her cell in the form of a giant; he tried for a long time to bite her, but being prevented by the power of God from tearing her in pieces, he seized her and dragged her furiously on the ground, till this chaste virgin entreated the protection of her Divine Spouse by these words of the royal prophet, "Lord, do not abandon to the tyrannical fury of these hellish monsters these who hope in Thee." Then the enemy immediately fled. Nothing occurs more frequently in the history of her life than the insults she received from the evil spirit. He appeared to her one day, and when she showed no fear of his malice, he gave her a severe blow on the cheek; another time he threw a great stone upon her from above, which struck her fainting to the ground.

One night when she was praying at home in a corner, she saw the devil in a large basket, making a horrible noise, to divert her from her application to God; she blew out the candle, and fortifying herself with the sign of the cross, she courageously challenged him to the combat; he accepted the offer, and changing his form in a moment, he appeared in the shape of a prodigious giant; he took hold of her by the shoulders and shook her as if he would tear her in pieces. She did not lose courage, and though her bones were almost broken, and her nerves relaxed by these rough shocks, she laughed at him, and reproached him with his weakness, that appearing so strong he could not even triumph over her firmness.

It was observed that she was very often engaged in combat

with the enemies of her salvation; and that whenever she was obliged to defend herself from their temptations, she was so intrepid that she never seemed to fear them, though they assumed horrible shapes, capable of freezing the blood in the veins of the boldest and most courageous persons: on the contrary, the more frightful they appeared, the more courageously did she attack them. She was once, however, obliged to change her method of defence, and gain the victory by flight on the following occasion:—The devil appeared to her one day in her garden, under the form of a beautiful young man; at the sight of this dangerous enemy, she retired without waiting or speaking to him; and by this flight she gained a complete and glorious victory, for taking a thick iron chain which she found, she gave herself a severe discipline; and then, covered with blood, she complained to her dear Spouse, that He had abandoned her on this occasion. Jesus Christ appeared to her immediately, surrounded with brightness, and consoling her, said, "Rose, thou art deceived, if thou imaginest that I left thee alone in this extremity; know that thou hast only avoided this danger by My grace, and that if I had not been with thee in this dangerous occasion, thou wouldst not have triumphed over the devil, who wished to surprise thee."

This incident in the life of our Saint is very similar to what happened to S. Catherine of Siena on one occasion. As Rose was no less cherished and favoured by God, He communicated to her, as well as to this seraphic lover, the gift of discernment, to distinguish the true revelations of God from the deceitful illusions of the spirit of darkness. God had bestowed this grace on her from her early youth, and from that time she prescribed infallible rules for the discernment of spirits, which she drew from the effects produced in souls by them. Jesus Christ had Himself taught them to S. Catherine of Siena, and this Saint too blessed Rose, who became so experienced, that if anyone in Peru had held Plato's opinions regarding the metempsychosis of souls, he would have believed that the soul of S. Catherine of Siena had passed into the body of Rose, her spiritual daughter and fervent disciple.

S. Catherine

CHAPTER XII

OF HER INVINCIBLE PATIENCE UNDER PERSECUTION IN SICKNESS, AND IN HER OTHER SUFFERINGS.

As thorns spring forth with roses, so grief and pain seem to have been born with the blessed Rose; for her life was a tissue of sufferings, sickness, pains, and crosses, which exercised her patience from her cradle to her tomb, by a long and tedious martyrdom. When Rose was only nine months old her mother lost her milk, and as she could not afford to pay for a nurse for her, she brought her up with a little broth instead of milk. Though the sweet child suffered greatly from this privation, and from the violence used in forcing open her mouth that she might take this nourishment, she never cried; on the contrary, she seemed to derive pleasure from it. We have spoken before of the wonderful patience she exhibited at the age of three months, under the painful operation of extracting the roots of her nail with pincers, when she did not shed a tear, but appeared as unmoved as if she were insensible to pain.

Scarcely had she begun to walk, when she saw herself the subject of a dispute between her mother and godmother, each wishing to call her by the name they had given her. Her mother would have her called Rose, and her godmother could not endure the idea of giving her any other name but that of Isabel, which she had received in baptism. Whatever this blessed child did was sure to offend one or the other. If she answered to the name of Isabel, her mother punished her severely; and when she wished to correct this innocent error by acknowledging the name of Rose, her godmother, who was also her aunt, treated her with the same rigour.

As she was of a mild disposition, quite opposite to the passionate temper of her mother, it would be difficult to describe all the harsh treatment she received from her during several years. Her mother found fault with everything she did; she condemned her reserve, she blamed her fasts, she did not like her taking up so much time in prayer, nor her retired life, so opposite to the maxims of the world; for these reasons she often scolded her, and went so far as to use many abusive epithets, as if she had been an infamous person. At the least provocation she gave her blows on the cheek, but when she was carried away by anger, she put no bounds to her ill-usage; she was not content with abusing her, striking her on the face, and kicking her; she took a thick knotty stick and struck her with it, with all her strength. She began to treat her thus when she cut off her hair after having consecrated her virginity to God, and she continued the same treatment on many other occasions.

These with whom she lived were actuated towards her by so extraordinary a spirit of envy and vexation, because they saw her lead a life so different from theirs, that they did everything they could to annoy her; they even threatened to report her to the Inquisition as a deluded girl and as a hypocrite, who deceived the world by a false appearance of virtue.

Rose blessed God under these persecutions; she suffered them with joy, as she had read in the life of her seraphic mistress that she also had attained a very close union with Jesus Christ by means of sufferings. When a lady of quality asked her why she did not beg S. Catherine of Siena to free her from these persecutions, for it was commonly said in Lima, that she obtained from God, by the intercession of this

Saint, whatever she asked for herself or others, she answered, "What would this dear mistress say to me, if I were to do so? Would she not have reason to reproach me, for choosing a different path from hers? Ah! May God preserve me from this cowardice!" In fact, our Saint esteemed the sufferings of S. Catherine of Siena more highly than her consolations; and she preferred the stigmas with which the Son of God honoured her to all the sweets of His caresses, because she thought it a shameful thing for a spouse of Jesus Christ crucified to be a moment without a cross.

She desired suffering with a sort of eagerness, and when Divine Providence sent her sickness to furnish her with an occasion of it, she felt much more compassion for the trouble she gave others who waited upon her, than pity for herself, which made her often say, " Oh how advantageous and agreeable it would be to be always ill and to suffer great pains, if we did not give so much trouble to these who attend upon us !" Almighty God, who inspired her with this great desire of sufferings, furnished her with many occasions for practising patience: she was scarcely ever one moment without suffering excessive pain, and when she had nothing to afflict her exteriorly, Almighty God sent her interior pains.

When these with whom she lived relaxed their unjust persecutions a little, sickness came upon her in all sorts of shapes. She was three years in bed a paralytic, suffering great torture without shedding a tear or making the least complaint. These diseases arose from different causes, which all united to increase her suffering. Even the physicians were surprised to see her suffer so long, sometimes from tertian, sometimes from quartan fevers, which made her burn with heat and then shiver with cold; for her body was so attenuated and dried up, that

there seemed to be scarcely anything remaining to nourish fever.

She on her part adored the Hand of God in her infirmities, acknowledging that they did not proceed in her from a derangement of the system, as is the case with others, but from the particular dispensation of her Divine Spouse, who sent them to exercise her patience and to furnish her with opportunities of merit and grace. She declared to one of her most familiar friends, that she did not think there was a member of her body that had not suffered all it was capable of enduring. Her patience was invincible in these continual sufferings, and though her pains sometimes rose to the highest degree of torture, she never showed a single movement of impatience, nor uttered a word of repugnance to follow the Will of God by this path of the cross; on the contrary, she always showed an entire resignation and readiness to suffer every thing she had to bear.

It is almost impossible to enumerate her different afflictions, for we think there are very few which she did not experience in the greatest degree. First she suffered long from a quinsy; secondly, she was subject to asthma, which impeded her respiration; thirdly, she felt for several years the severe pains of sciatica, which tormented her day and night; fourthly, she was several times in danger from pleurisy; fifthly, she frequently fell into convulsions caused by the pain she suffered in the membrane which surrounds the heart; sixthly, she was scarcely ever free from fever; seventhly, we must confess that she stood in need of all her patience to bear the pain of gout in her hands and feet, and though this affliction is generally the effect and the punishment of intemperance, this chaste virgin was cruelly tormented by it, although her whole life had been spent in fasting and severe penitential exercises.

In all these violent pains, which succeeded one another, and which made the blessed Rose a daughter of affliction, she made known to those whom she saw touched with compassion for her sufferings, that she was still too well, that Almighty God treated her with too much tenderness, and that if He were to increase her pains to an infinite degree, He would do her no injustice, for she had deserved more. In the extremity of her sufferings she turned lovingly towards her crucifix, from which she derived her strength and patience, and addressed her Divine Redeemer in these tender and affectionate words, " O, my Jesus! O, my Jesus! Increase my sufferings, but increase also Thy Divine love in my soul!" We may conjecture from a vision which she had one day, that the Son of God heard the ardent prayers of this chaste spouse. He appeared to her on two very brilliant rainbows, holding a pair of golden scales, in which He weighed on one side the sufferings mankind could endure, and on the other the graces and infinite rewards which He promises; she heard Him immediately extol with magnificent praises the constancy of these who suffer generously for His love, and declare aloud that there was no other way of mounting to heaven but by the ladder of the cross.

This vision inflamed her heart with so great a desire of suffering all things for His Divine love, that she wished to go and publish to all men the inestimable advantages of affliction, and the great grace which God bestows whenever He sends sickness, losses, or any other visitation; for these apparent evils acquire for these who bear them an infinity of merits, which dispose them for the possession of sovereign happiness. The blessed Rose drew new strength from this vision, and encouragement under the paralytic seizure, which Almighty God sent to crown her patience, and which caused her to die as it were a martyr in the flower of her age.

CHAPTER XIII

OF HER LOVE FOR HER DIVINE SPOUSE JESUS CHRIST, AND OF THE MIRACLE WHICH SHE ENTREATED HIM TO WORK TO INFLAME THE HEARTS OF MEN WITH HIS DIVINE LOVE.

As charity makes saints, Almighty God, who destined S. Rose to attain a high degree of sanctity, rendered her heart, as it were, another Etna, which sent forth night and day flames of love, and which was so completely filled with this celestial fire, that the heat and sparks from it were visible on her countenance during her prayer. Fire was frequently seen issuing from her mouth and eyes, and through them she was enabled to give vent to the flames with which she was consumed while conversing with God by prayer. The ardent sighs which she continually breathed, manifested this evidently, for she was obliged to allow them to escape her, in order to moderate the violent heat of the love which burnt in her heart

This burning charity pervaded so completely all the faculties of her soul, that nothing issued from her heart, her mouth, or eyes, that did not express this celestial ardour. She had almost continually these words in her mouth, " Oh, my God ! who would not love Thee? Oh, good Jesus when shall I begin to love Thee, as I ought? How far am I from this perfect, intimate, and generous love? Alas! I know not even how to love Thee. How shameful! Of what advantage is it to have a heart, unless it be quite consumed with the love of Thee!" Inflamed with this divine charity, she composed several ejaculatory prayers, to obtain this perfect love of God, which are so moving that they might produce in the hearts of these who read them the same effects as in the heart of our Saint. The following is an example:

"Lord Jesus Christ, God and Man, my Creator and my Saviour, I am extremely sorry and sensibly grieved for having offended Thee, because Thou art what Thou art, and because I love Thee above all things. My God, Who art the Spouse of my soul and all the joy of my heart, I desire, and I desire it with all the powers of my soul, to love Thee with a very perfect love, with a very efficacious love, with a very sincere, ineffable love, the greatest that a creature can have for her God, with an incomprehensible love, with a love resolute and invincible in difficulties; in a word, I desire to love Thee as the saints and angels love Thee in heaven. Even more, O God of my heart, of my life, and all the joy of my soul, I desire to love Thee, as far as I am capable of it; as much as the Blessed Virgin, Thy Mother and my sweet Lady, loves Thee. O Salvation of my Soul! I desire to love Thee as Thou lovest Thyself. O my most sweet Jesus may I burn with the fire of Thy divine love; may it consume me, and make of my soul a holocaust to Thy glory."

She was so penetrated with this love, that it was the ordinary subject of her conversations with others; for whenever she spoke with ladies or with young girls, she always began by thesewords, " Let us love God, let us love Him With all our hearts."We may say, in a word, that the love of God was the salt with which she seasoned all her words, either in conversation, in answering questions, or when civility obliged her to speak to anyone.

All her pleasure was in speaking of this love, or in hearing others speak of it, and when anything else was made the subject of discourse in her presence, she contrived to turn the conversation, and to make it almost imperceptibly fall upon the excellence of charity, and on the happy necessity in which we are of loving God with all our soul, and with all our strength. She spoke very little, but on this occasion she was wonderfully eloquent. It was easy to perceive by the fire that sparkled in her eyes that in these delightful discourses on the love of God her tongue was the faithful interpreter of her heart, and that she drew from the abundance of the charity with which it was replenished the substance of everything she said.

It was delightful to hear her when praying in her hermitage, giving full scope to her love, and exhorting all creatures to love God, who had given them their being. She generally remained two or three hours in these transports, and these who observed her closely sometimes saw her take a harp, and joining the sweetness of her beautiful voice to the symphony of that instrument, she sang canticles of praise to God for His love towards men. As divine love is a fire, it cannot be so concealed in the soul as not sometimes to manifest its presence by actions of piety, to which the soul is impelled by the desire of pleasing God. S. Rose, reflecting one day on the charity which S. Catherine of Siena had shown towards Jesus Christ, hidden under the form of a beggar, in depriving herself of her garments to clothe Him, thought she might imitate her by making a sort of spiritual and mysterious garment for the Infant Jesus of several acts of virtue. This is the formula which was found in her own handwriting:

<h2 style="text-align:center">" Jesus.</h2>

"This year, 1616, by the grace of my Saviour, and under the protection of the Blessed Virgin Mary, I will clothe my Divine Jesus, whom the Church will soon represent to us born naked in a manger, exposed to all the severity of winter. I will make him an under garment of fifty Litanies, of nine hundred chaplets, which

I will recite, and of five days of abstinence from every sort of nourishment, in honour of the adorable mystery of the Incarnation. I will compose His swaddling clothes of nine visits to the most Blessed Sacrament, of nine Psalters of the Blessed Virgin, and of nine fasting days, to honour the nine months during which He was enclosed in her chaste womb. His covering shall consist of five days passed without eating or drinking, of five visits to the most Blessed Sacrament, and of as many Rosaries, in honour of His birth in this world. His bands shall be made of three chaplets of our Lord, of three days' abstinence from food, and of five stations which I will make before the most Blessed Sacrament. For the fringes and borders of His swaddling clothes and bands, I will make thirty-three extra communions, I will assist at thirty-three masses, I will spend thirty- three hours in mental prayer, I will recite thirty- three times the Pater Noster, thirty-three times the Ave Maria, Credo, Gloria Patri, and Salve Regina; I will also recite thirty-three Rosaries, I will fast thirty-three days, I will take three thousand stripes of the discipline, in honour of the thirty-three years He spent on earth. Lastly, I offer as a gift to my dear Jesus, my tears, my sighs, and all the acts of love which I shall make. With this I offer my heart and soul, that there may be nothing in me which is not entirely consecrated to Him."

Zeal being the fruit of love, draws its degrees of excellence from the cause which gives birth to it; so that if love be imperfect, zeal is cold and languishing : on the contrary, if love be generous, zeal is all on fire; thus, as the love of God which consumed the soul of S. Rose was most ardent, she had an incomparable zeal for His glory.

There was no one in the house bold enough to say one word in her presence contrary to modesty: they well knew that her generous zeal for the interests of God would prompt her to condemn it instantly. She could not endure a word to be spoken in the church, much less that it should be made a place for conversation; her zeal, closing her eyes to human respect and every consideration of flesh and blood, gave her a holy confidence in speaking to anyone whatever, who committed this act of irreverence. From her youth upwards, when she heard her brothers and sisters sing profane airs or immodest verses, she wept for grief, and showed them by the abundance of her tears how much the freedom of their words wounded her heart. She must indeed have felt it exceedingly, for she had so high an esteem for tears, which she said belonged to the treasury of God, and were a useful sort of money, with which we may purchase the kingdom of heaven, that she could not endure their being wasted for any earthly cause; hence, seeing her mother shedding them one day profusely for trifles, she said, " Ah mother! why do you waste this precious merchandise, which you might deposit in the treasury of God to avail towards your salvation?"

This zeal made her enter so deeply into the interests of her Divine Spouse, that she felt an incredible joy when she saw Him served and honoured by men; and a poor nun having returned to her convent after having scandalously left it, our Saint showed more pleasure on this occasion than if the crown of all America had been placed on her head; and God, to increase her joy, showed her in spirit the eminent sanctity which this repentant religious would attain through her tears and sighs. Her confessor having been requested to preach on some considerable occasion, when all the chief people in the town would be present, was attacked with a violent fever. Rose, being acquainted with his indisposition, very earnestly begged of Almighty God to send her the fever from which her confessor was suffering. In the confidence she felt that her prayer would be heard, she sent to tell him to prepare for this great action, for he would certainly be without fever when he entered the pulpit, which happened according to her desires, and be acquitted himself of this honourable employment greatly to the satisfaction of his hearers, while S. Rose was suffering the burning heats of his fever.

Almighty God testified His approbation of the eagerness of S. Rose in advancing His glory by a celebrated miracle. In 1617, the year in which she died, on the 15th of April, about five o'clock in the evening, as she was praying in the oratory of Don Gonzalez before a very beautiful statue of Jesus Christ, she felt so ardent a love of God, that, unable to moderate its violence, she rose up and began to address Him, and after some devout colloquies, she begged Him to enkindle the fire of His love in the hearts of men. At the same instant in which she made this prayer, the daughter of Don Gonzalez perceived that this image of the Son of God was quite moist with perspiration, by which He made known, in order to satisfy Rose's desire, the immensity of His charity for men, that being convinced of it by this prodigy, they might detach their affections from creatures, to consecrate them to Him and to love Him only.

Don Gonzalez hurried to the place when he heard of the miracle, and seeing the image sweat, he sent immediately for the Rev. Fathers Diego Martinez, and Diego Penalosa, that they might be eyewitnesses of this prodigy. The first being prevented, the second came, and having entered the oratory, he saw the sweat, and wiped it off himself with cotton. He perceived that this miraculous appearance augmented in proportion as he wiped it. This miracle lasted four hours, in the presence of a number of persons of consideration, whom this prodigy had drawn to the place. They saw several drops of perspiration, as large as little beads, rise successively on the face of this statue one after the other, and run down the hair and neck: the more they wiped the more abundant did the sweat

become, but it did not injure the colours of the painting; on the contrary, it seemed like a varnish which gave them additional brightness. Don Barthelemy Lobo Guerrero, then Archbishop of Lima, appointed Dr. Juan de la Roca, curate and archdeacon of the metropolitan church, judge to examine it juridically. When the examination had been made, and the depositions of the witnesses had been taken, this sweat was declared to be miraculous, not proceeding from the coldness of the place, nor from the unctuous moisture of the oil, with which the colours used in painting the statue had been mixed, but that it was an effect of the omnipotence of God, who acts when He pleases, out of the order of nature and above the rules of art.

Don Gonzalez was very uneasy about this; he feared that this prodigy might be a forerunner of the justice of God, Who intended, perhaps, to punish some secret sin, committed by some member of his family: but S. Rose removed his fear, telling him that Jesus Christ in this image had sweated to animate mankind to love Him. This miracle, which so sweetly invited men to love God, accomplished the charitable desire of our Saint, for all these who had ocular demonstration of it felt an internal fire, inflaming them with the ardour of the charity of Jesus Christ, and were happily pierced with the darts of His divine love. This miracle gave rise to another, for S. Rose having seriously injured herself by a fall, the surgeons feared she would die, or at least be a cripple the rest of her life; but she, having more confidence in the goodness of God than in the efficacy of remedies, thought that she should certainly be cured if she were to dip a little cotton in the sweat of that image, and apply it to her wounded arm; but from the delight she felt in suffering, she dared not do it without speaking first to her confessor, and obtaining his permission. He wished her to follow the first inspiration, believing that Almighty God had sent it, in order to manifest His power by some new miracle. As soon as she applied this moistened cotton to her arm, she felt the nerves return to their place, the cartilages grow stronger, the tumour sink down, and the muscles stretch out. This was a source of astonishment to the surgeons who despaired of curing this evil.

She sends her guardian angel

CHAPTER XIV

OF HER DEVOTION TOWARDS THE MOST BLESSED SACRAMENT, IN DEFENCE OF WHICH SHE ONCE PREPARED HERSELF TO SUFFER MARTYRDOM

If the union of the soul with God be the principle of its happiness and of its progress in virtue, it necessarily follows that devotion towards the most Holy Sacrament of the altar is the most efficacious means of arriving in a short time at perfection and sanctity. From this inexhaustible source of grace S. Rose drew strength, light, and heat; through this sacred channel Almighty God communicated Himself intimately to her, and, in fine, it was by the frequent use of this adorable mystery, that possessing God fully in herself, she was enabled to say with S. Paul, that she lived no longer a natural and human life, but that Jesus Christ her Divine Spouse lived in her, since the grace of this august Sacrament had quite transformed her into Him.

She communicated regularly three times a week, frequently five times, and in some circumstances of her life she communicated every day, according to the orders given her by these who regulated her conscience. As this Divine Sacrament operates according to the dispositions of the receiver, S. Rose prepared for it by confession, which she frequented not by routine, as many in the world do who profess devotion, and who confess their imperfections without any sorrow for them, but with a contrite heart, trying to blot out her sins by a river of tears, and to obtain pardon from the mercy of God by her

sighs. On the eve of her communion she fasted rigorously, on bread and water usually, and took the discipline to blood, and by these austerities she sought to imitate Jesus Christ her Spouse, who is immolated as a victim in this mystery.

She had also the holy custom of preparing her heart for Him by a number of ejaculatory prayers, to express the loving impatience she felt to possess Him; in a word, she disposed herself as carefully for each communion, as if she were going to enjoy that happiness for the last time in her life. Every time she communicated she was so transported with love, that the fire of charity which consumed her soul showed itself on her countenance, and made it appear so beautiful, and sometimes so bright, that even the priests were seized with awe and fear when they brought the Sacred Host to communicate her. She was often surrounded with light at the altar; sometimes she seemed to possess a superhuman beauty; and these who noticed this change would have taken her for an angel, had not her face resumed its ordinary expression; and many religious persons have attested, that when she was making her thanksgiving after communion, they saw issue from her eyes, her hands, and almost every part of her body, rays as brilliant as these of the sun.

Her confessors sometimes obliged her to declare the admirable effects which this adorable Sacrament operated in her soul; she obeyed, but at each word she stopped short, finding it difficult to express the sentiments of her mind, and what passed in her interior; nevertheless to give them some faint idea of these things, she told them, that her heart, her mind, and her whole self became, as it were, transported into God; that she experienced such excessive joy, that all the pleasures of the earth were not to be compared to these she tasted in this magnificent banquet, where Almighty God seems to make these whom He admits to it partakers in His happiness and in His divinity. She declared to them also, that she found in it an entire satiety; and that she derived from it such extraordinary strength, that though before communion she was quite weak from fasting, and from the loss of the blood which she drew from her veins by disciplines, so that she was sometimes obliged to rest in the middle of the church, not being able to go as far as the altar without taking breath, she went from the holy table with the same strength as the prophet Elias felt after having eaten bread baked in the ashes, which was the symbol of the blessed Eucharist, and of the strength which it communicates to these who receive it.

Those belonging to the family have borne witness, that the satiety which she found in the sacred table replenished her so completely, that she shut herself up in her room or in her hermitage without taking any nourishment, and that she remained there till night, and often till the next day, devoutly occupied and quite enraptured in the chaste embraces of her Divine Spouse. And when they called or came to seek her at the time of meals, she, who had fasted the day before, excused herself, saying, it was impossible for her to take anything; so that she was sometimes known to fast eight whole days; and, in imitation of S. Catherine of Siena, to take no other food than that which she had received at the banquet of angels in the holy communion. On her communion days she assisted at every mass that was said till noon with such great recollection, that she kept her eyes always fixed on the altar, and though a great number of persons passed and re-passed continually before her, she saw no one.

When the forty hours' prayer was taking place in any church, she went thither, and remained motionless before the most Holy Sacrament, completely absorbed in God from morning till night. She thought not of food or drink, and though the excessive heat of the country required that she should assuage her thirst with a little water, she felt in her heart a fire of love more vehement than that which heated her body, and this made her forget her necessary refreshment. The following was her method of proceeding during the Octave of the most Blessed Sacrament, and the manner in which she spent the four last years of her life. She was not satisfied with accompanying the Beloved of her heart in procession to the sepulchre on Maundy Thursday, she remained in His company for twenty-four hours, with such profound respect that she dared not sit, nor even lean ever so little against the wall, to support her extreme weakness. Anyone who saw her standing motionless, bathed in tears, now and then looking towards heaven and sighing in the bitterness of her heart, would have taken her for another Magdalen, inseparably attached to the sepulchre of her dear Master by the invisible chains of his love. When the most Blessed Sacrament was carried through the town to the sick, she felt so transported with joy at the sound of the bell, that this interior gladness pervaded her whole body. At the sight of her God, she knelt down wherever she was, and after having adored Him prostrate on the earth, she accompanied Him to the sick, and followed Him to the church with unspeakable satisfaction, thinking herself infinitely happy on these occasions of offering her homage to the Son of God, her Sovereign Lord.

She took great pleasure in washing the church linen, and in making and repairing neatly everything connected with the decoration of the altar. She made flowers of gold and silk for this purpose; and for fear that the time which she spent in these works of piety might prevent her from helping her family, who partly depended on her labours for a living, she devoted part of the night to them, taking away the hours from her sleep to consecrate them to the embellishment of the house of God. Her love for the adorable mystery of the altar was so generous, that she resolved once to defend it from the rage of heretics at the expense of her blood and life; for in her fear that they would get possession of the Blessed Sacrament, and make it the subject of profanation and sacrilege, she ran to the church to oppose their violence by force, though she could not doubt that they would despise her resistance, and tear her in pieces if she attempted to oppose their design.

It happened as follows: in the month of August, 1615, a powerful fleet of the States-General of Holland appeared on the coasts of Peru. Already the vanguard of the enemy was seen approaching the port of Lima, and the greater part of the ships belonging to this naval armament coasted so near the land, that some merchants of Lima, whom this fleet had taken by surprise, thought they saw the boats of the admiral's ship and of the other vessels put on land a quantity of soldiers. Every one was in tears; nothing was heard but the cries of women and children; and the men prepared to defend themselves in such confusion and disorder, that nothing could be expected but the total ruin of the country. Rose, who did not only look upon these heretics as the enemies of her country, but chiefly as the mortal enemies of Jesus Christ, thought of nothing in this general consternation but of defending the most Blessed Sacrament at the peril of her life, for It was exposed in all the churches of the town. She animated her companions, and exhorted them to die generously for the defence of this most august Mystery. With the resolution of suffering herself to be slain by these soldiers, she disposed herself to resist their violence courageously; she mounted on the steps of the altar with the same resolution as S. Ambrose represents Judith to have shown in approaching the camp of the enemies of God. Rose knew very well that she could not resist the violence of these who would put her to death; but she prepared to fight, to honour the belief in this great Sacrament.

From her sparkling eyes, her proud air, and the tone of her voice, which was that of a heroine exhorting the troops to combat, she might have been taken for a Christian Minerva, armed for the defence of religion, or for an angry lioness, which rushes on against the weapons of the hunters, who are carrying away its little ones. She was found in this state of preparation and resolution to die on the steps of the altar by the hand of these heretical soldiers, when news was brought that the fleet had weighed anchor, and sailed away without any manifestation of hostility. Everywhere in Lima the people were heard blessing God; each one expressed his joy and gratitude; Rose alone seemed inconsolable in this general delight, for she grieved to have lost the opportunity of martyrdom which she had thought so near. She had so earnest a desire of dying a martyr, that she every day asked of Almighty God the grace of shedding her blood, and of dying by the hand of a sacrilegious person or an executioner. She often regretted that she was not born in these times when tyrants cruelly massacred the Christians, thinking that then she should not have failed to lose her life for Jesus Christ.

This desire of martyrdom, which neither the peace of the Church, nor the little prospect she saw of being exposed to the persecution of heretics and infidels, could extinguish in her heart, often made her say, with tears in her eyes, "Would to God that I could find the opportunity and the means of going to distant pagan countries, that I might die by the hands of barbarians for Jesus Christ my dear Spouse."

CHAPTER XV

OF HER DEVOTION TO AN IMAGE OF OUR BLESSED LADY, TO THE SIGN OF THE CROSS, AND TO HER DEAR MISTRESS S. CATHERINE OF SIENA

For more than a century the people of the town of Lima had honoured a statue of the Blessed Virgin in the church of the Friars Preachers, under the name of Our Lady of the Rosary, a devotion which these monks had taught to the people at the time that they planted the faith in the most celebrated provinces of America.

But before we speak of the graces which S. Rose received by this means, we must go farther back, and show what rendered the people so devout to this image.

It was a wooden statue of our Blessed Lady, five feet high, which the first Spanish Christians who passed over into Peru with our forefathers brought from Europe with them, to be the powerful Protectress of their project. She holds the Infant Jesus with her left arm, and with the right hand offers a Rosary. When they had settled in this country, and had built this famous town now called Lima, they raised a superb church for the religious of the Order of Friars Preachers, under the name of the Holy Rosary, which was the first church and the first parish in which baptismal fonts were erected for the regeneration of spiritual children to Jesus Christ in the New World; and they placed in it this image, which was honoured

by the people with special veneration, on account of the signal favours received through the protection of the Blessed Virgin of the Holy Rosary.

The year 1535 was marked by one of these instances of her patronage. The Indians had assembled near Caxaguana, in the province of Cusco, to the number of two hundred thousand, in order to massacre the Christians; and they felt the more assured of victory as the Spanish army opposed to them consisted only of six hundred men. In this consternation the religious, having placed themselves at the head of the Christian troops, exhorted them to implore the protection of our Lady of the Holy Rosary. They did so, and, filled with confidence in her assistance, they gave battle to this great multitude of Indians. At the moment in which the engagement began, they perceived in the air the Blessed Virgin, under the same form as she is represented in the Church of the Rosary, holding a rod in her hand, and threatening the Indians with death if they did not withdraw. The infidels were so alarmed at this vision, and so dazzled with the splendour that surrounded the Blessed Virgin, that they begged for quarter, and submitted not only to Spain, but also to the yoke of Jesus Christ by becoming Christians. This memorable victory greatly increased the devotion of the people towards our Lady of the Rosary.

Philip IV, King of Spain, having placed his kingdom of Peru under the protection of the Blessed Virgin on the 27th May, 1643, and having given notice of his intention to the archbishop, the viceroy, and magistrates of Lima, exhorted them to choose some image of the Blessed Virgin, and address to it their prayers, that they might obtain succour from her in the dangers which threatened the country. When the orders of his Catholic majesty were received, the archbishop, the viceroy, and the two estates ecclesiastical and secular, chose our Lady of the Rosary to be the Protectress of the whole kingdom of

Peru, and resolved that the people should every year go in procession, on the Monday in Low Week, to the church of the Friars Preachers, to offer their prayers to her. This procession took place every year with great pomp; the image of our Lady was carried from the church through the town, the garrison being under arms; the chapter of the cathedral, the religious, the viceroy, the officers and magistrates assisted at it. The devotion towards this image was so great, that every day a crowd of people came to pray before it.

S. Rose spent some time every day in prayer on her knees before the altar on which this image was placed, with very great devotion, which increased more and more in her heart, as she perceived that this inanimate statue cast towards her looks of tenderness, and made certain signs as if it wished to caress her, and manifest to her by these miraculous movements, the love which the Blessed Virgin, of whom it was but the copy, bore to her. She noticed the same affability in the face of the Infant Jesus whom this image was represented as holding; she too saw Him sometimes smile, extending His arms to caress her, and He gave her so many visible signs that He answered the love which she bore Him, that she felt as certain of it as if she had seen His affection for her painted or engraved in large letters. It seemed to her that this Divine Infant wished to leave His Mother to throw Himself into her arms, in order to caress her with greater facility. It was looked upon in the town as certain that Rose obtained whatever she asked of Heaven when she prayed before this image, and she herself felt as sure of obtaining what she asked through the intercession of our Lady of the Rosary, as if she had received from Heaven letters patent, confirming all the graces she requested for herself or for others.

She was also very devout to another image of the Blessed Virgin, which she honoured particularly in her oratory at home, because she had remarked that this image gave signs of life, that it changed its position, approached her, smiled upon her, and offered her the same caresses as if it were truly the Blessed Virgin, and not a mere copy of the original. When a lady, who had come to see her, was relating in the presence of this image the great miracles which the Blessed Virgin worked every day at Achota, a place of devotion near Madrid in Spain, in favour of these devout persons who came to honour her, and of the sick who sought her protection to obtain from God the cure of their diseases, Rose remarked, during this conversation, that her image gave great signs of joy, looked at her with a smiling countenance, and shone more brightly than usual.

Every Saturday she took care to adorn the Chapel of the Rosary with flowers which she had cultivated expressly for this purpose. She was never known to fail in this act of devotion; and in summer, when the heat of the sun dries up all the plants, as well as in winter, when the cold renders gardens unproductive, the altar was seen as richly ornamented with flowers as in the time of spring. She had also undertaken to adorn with a robe this image, to which she had so great a devotion; but the spiritual garment which she composed of her prayers, her fasts, her disciplines, her tears, and of all the acts of virtue she practised, as an ornament for the Queen of Heaven, was much more pleasing to her than if she had clothed her with some costly material. The following is the method she practised, which she wrote down herself:—

" JESUS, MARY.

"The spiritual garment which I, Sister Rose of S. Mary, unworthy servant of the Queen of Angels, prepare, by her help, for the Blessed Virgin, Mother of God. 1st, her tunic shall consist of six hundred Ave Marias, as many Salve Reginas, and of fifteen fasting days, in honour of the spiritual joy which she felt in her holy soul when the Archangel announced to her the Incarnation of the Word in her chaste womb. 2ndly, the material for this mysterious robe shall be six hundred Ave Marias, six hundred Salve Reginas, fifteen

Rosaries, and fifteen fasting days, in honour of the joy she felt in going to visit her cousin S. Elizabeth. 3rdly, I will border it with six hundred Ave Marias, as many Salve Reginas, fifteen Rosaries, and fifteen fasting days, in honour of the joy which filled her heart when the Son of God was born into the world. 4thly, The clasps shall be made of six hundred Ave Marias, of six hundred Salve Reginas, and fifteen fasting days, in honour of her interior joy in offering her Son Jesus Christ in the Temple. 5thly, her necklace shall be composed of six hundred Ave Marias, as many Salves, of fifteen fasting days, and fifteen Rosaries, in honour of that joy she felt in finding her Son in the Temple, in the midst of the doctors, three days after having lost Him. 6thly, the sceptre that I shall place in her hand shall be made of thirty-three Paters, thirty-three Rosaries, thirty-three Gloria Patris, and thirty-three Salve Reginas, in honour of the thirty-three years which Jesus Christ, God and Man, lived on earth for our salvation." A little below she wrote: —"May God be eternally glorified, and His most pure Mother, the Virgin Mary, honoured by every creature! I have made this spiritual garment, and have acquitted myself of this devotion, by the help of the grace of my God, who has supplied for my defects."

She had a wonderful devotion to the sign of the cross; she kissed every day a large wooden cross, which she had in her cell in the garden, with such tender sentiments of love and respect, that it was easy to see that she bore its mysteries deeply engraved in her heart. Wherever she saw a cross, she knelt down to venerate it. She had the same respect for every thing which bore the figure of a cross; for when she saw any likeness of it, in pieces of wood placed across, or in the interwoven branches of trees or hedges, or in pieces of straw, or in the bolts of doors, she felt herself interiorly moved by the form of the sign of our salvation, and never passed on without showing marks of respect and veneration. Amongst the plants and flowers which she cultivated in her father's garden, she had a large rosemary, the principal branches of which formed a cross. The wife of the viceroy of Peru asked her for one of them; not being able to refuse so small a gift to a lady of her merit and quality, she sent her one, but as soon as it was planted in her garden it died. Rose's confessor having told her of it, she answered that it was not to be wondered at; for the cross cannot exist amongst the delights and vanities of the court.

The Marquess of Salinas del Río Pisuerga, 8th Viceroy of Peru

She begged that it might be sent back to her, and having replanted it, in four days it was as green and beautiful as ever.

The members of the Confraternity of S. Catherine of Siena were accustomed to carry her image round the town every year, adorned with a crown of flowers and precious stones. Rose, who honoured her as her dear mistress, and loved her as her spiritual mother, could not bear that anyone else should render her this service; she contrived so well, that she was charged with the duty of carrying it, and she acquitted herself of it, as long as she lived, with great sentiments of tenderness and devotion. Besides this commission she had obtained also the appointment of sacristan to her chapel; she adorned her image as richly as she could, but with so tender a devotion, that in doing this she gave it a thousand kisses, and expressed to her by ardent words the love she had for her. "O my dear mistress," said she one day, " how I regret not to have money to clothe you with another garment!" As she finished speaking, a slave of Madame Hierome de Gama brought her the money she had desired for this pious design.

One day in May, which is the season of winter in the torrid zone, when she wished to adorn her as usual, she went to seek flowers in her garden, but not finding any, she commanded a root of pinks to furnish her with some, and immediately there

appeared several beautiful flowers, though there had not been any ready to come out before. She gathered in the same manner a quantity of roses from a rose tree. This miracle happened so frequently that it no longer caused surprise to the people of Lima and the surrounding country. It was not without reason that she honoured with special devotion the image of this seraphic virgin; she had often seen her surrounded with heavenly light, and had been present at the miracle she worked in curing Frances de Montoya, by preserving her from the effects of a sulphurous flame which would have caused the loss of her eye, without this miraculous assistance. She had herself experienced the effects of the goodness and power of her dear mistress, when she was suffering from gout, which had swelled her hands so much that she could not move her fingers.

In the year 1616, S. Rose wishing to adorn her image to carry it in procession on the feast of S. Dominic, which was drawing near, begged her to enable her to continue the performance of her usual duties. After her prayer she put her fingers within the rings of her scissors without reflecting on her infirmity, and from the size to which her fingers were swollen she could not have done this without a miracle. This assistance, which her good mistress gave her, filled her with joy, and greatly surprised the Receiver, his wife, and several physicians, who confessed that it was an effect of the Divine Power, which bad cured her in an instant.

S. Catherine of Siena by Andrea di Vanni, one of her disciples.

CHAPTER XVI

OF HER ZEAL FOR THE SALVATION OF SOULS, AND HER CARE IN ASSISTING THE POOR IN THEIR SICKNESS AND NECESSITIES.

True love being always accompanied by zeal, it follows that we cannot perfectly love the Son of God, who takes so great an interest in the salvation of these souls whom He has redeemed with His Precious Blood, without being also zealous for the eternal welfare of sinners for whom He suffered death. As this zeal was the characteristic of S. Dominic, and as it still inflames the hearts of these among her children whom the

Church destines to gain souls, we need not be surprised that S. Rose, his beloved daughter, should have received the spirit of zeal of this great patriarch with the habit of his Order. She showed during her whole life an indefatigable zeal for the conversion of sinners, and never failed one single day to ask of God for them by her prayers, and generally also by her  blood, the grace to be restored to His friendship.

Whenever she cast her eyes on the high mountains of South America, she wept for the eternal loss of the barbarous people who dwelt amongst them. Her zeal being as boundless as her charity, she deplored also the damnation of the almost innumerable multitude of pagans in the New World, who have no knowledge of God, nor of the adorable mysteries of religion; she desired to be torn in pieces, and placed at the gate of hell, as a barrier to hinder men from precipitating themselves into it, as they do every day.

She exhorted religious persons, whenever she met them, in words of fire, to go and preach the Gospel to the idolatrous Indians, warning them especially to shun studied figures of rhetoric, which corrupt the purity of the word of God; and not to be attached to the useless subtleties of the schools, nor to the questions which are therein agitated, unless they may be useful in converting infidels. She sometimes said, in a transport of zeal, that if Almighty God had made her of a different sex, she would have applied herself to study, in order to labour with all her power for the conversion of souls, and that when her studies were finished she would have penetrated into the most distant provinces and most barbarous nations of America, to enlighten these savages with the torch of faith, or to finish her life by a  glorious martyrdom. Seeing herself incapacitated by her sex from executing this charitable design, she had resolved to adopt a child, and bring him up to study and prayer, by the help of the alms given her and the money she gained by her work, that she might send him to preach to infidels when he was capable of it.

One of her confessors being undecided about accompanying some good religious in a mission to the Indians, for which they were preparing, she made over to him half the merit she might have gained by the good works which she had performed by the grace of God, in order to animate him to this enterprise, in which the salvation of a great number of souls was in question. If she had great zeal for these poor Indians, what shall we say of that which she manifested for the salvation of Christians, who are, as S. Paul says, of the household of the faith, when she saw them in danger of losing heaven by their crimes and excesses?

She took every day severe disciplines for their conversion; and as she could not keep to herself the zeal which inflamed her, she sometimes made it known by these words: "Ah, if it were permitted to me to exercise the function of preacher, I would go by day and by night barefoot into the most public places, covered with a hair-shirt, and bearing a large cross on my shoulders, to exhort sinners to do penance, and to represent to them the fearful severity of the judgments of God." And she modestly advised these who were engaged in the apostolical ministry, to make these subjects the ordinary matter of their discourses, to renounce the ornaments of worldly rhetoric, and to abstain from these studied declamations, which are more suited to the theatre than to the pulpit, because preachers are established by Almighty God to be fishers of men, that is, to withdraw them from sin and hell by their fervent exhortations.

She was animated with the spirit of her father S. Dominic, and would have considered herself to have degenerated from the glorious quality of his daughter, if she had not imitated his ardent charity for others; therefore all her aim was to draw men to God, to bring them from vice, and to inspire them with a love for virtue. She never spoke with anyone without leading the conversation to the necessity of knowing, loving, and serving God, and to the obligation contracted by every Christian of leading a holy life, of renouncing the maxims and vanities of the world, and of clothing themselves with Jesus Christ by an imitation of these virtues which He practised for our example. She was so thoroughly persuaded of the truths she uttered, and so deeply touched by them, that she scarcely

spoke to any person without gaining him to God, and inducing him to change his life.

Almighty God often made use of her in a miraculous manner for the conversion of several persons engaged in vice. A young man of high family, but whose life did not correspond with his noble blood, despairing of marrying Rose, whom he passionately loved, sought at least some comfort in the pleasure of seeing her; he watched carefully for opportunities; he gained her mother over, and agreed with her that she should order Rose to make collars and linen for him, which he pretended to want. When her mother called her to speak to him, and to accompany him to the linen draper's shop, Almighty God made known to Rose the evil intention of this young gentleman, whose name was Don Vincent Montelis Venergas. Thus warned by heaven, she met him with civility, spoke to him strongly, and filled him with so great a fear of the judgments of God, that he left her entirely converted, and so touched with what she had said, that he, giving himself wholly to God, and applying himself diligently to the care of his salvation, he lived from that time in sentiments of exemplary piety, and generally communicated every week.

She contributed no less to the salvation of a woman, whose passionate temper caused her to fall into such excesses of impatience every minute, that it was impossible to live with her and to have a quarter of an hour's peace. She went one day to visit S. Rose in her cell, and this holy virgin made her a discourse on the meekness which the Son of God has taught us by His words and example; and she showed her so efficaciously the excellence and necessity of this virtue, which is, in some degree, the spirit of Christianity, that this woman overcame her fiery and passionate temper, telling every one that she had been delighted with the admonitions of our Saint, and that the sweetness of her eyes and words always extinguished in her the impetuous sallies of anger, to which her temper and a long indulged habit gave rise continually in her heart.

S. Rose's confessor, Father Peter of Louysa, knowing the greatness of her compassionate zeal, informed her that a certain religious was suffering dreadful pains; in his agony he was seen to sweat, shudder, and tremble with a lively apprehension of the rigour of God's judgments. She begged this good father to fortify him and to animate him to hope by the representation of the boundless mercy of Almighty God; and to offer him from her a part of all the good she had done during her life in the service of God, in order to supply what might be wanting to him before he could enter heaven; and to tell him that she should be glad to know the state of his soul after death, that she might continue her prayers and suffrages for him if he stood in need of them, he was greatly comforted by S. Rose's charity, and died in great tranquillity. Some days after Almighty God revealed to her that the soul of this person was in possession of eternal happiness.

It will perhaps appear

surprising, and not without cause, that the funeral of S. Rose should have been honoured with the cries, tears, and sighs of the poor, and that they should have been heard bitterly to lament having lost, in the person of Rose, their mother and their nurse, since she was so poor herself, and so ill provided with the goods of this life, that she was obliged to support her family partly by her own work; nevertheless, we need not be astonished at it, if we reflect that charity is powerful, and the zeal which accompanies it ingenious in devising means to help others in their necessities. She assisted them, first, by begging for them in the first houses in the town, where her virtue made her well received, and where the distribution of plentiful alms was confided to her. Secondly, by liberally dividing with them the charity which was given her for herself, as it was known that she had to support her parents and family. Thirdly, by depriving herself of the necessaries of life to help them. In this spirit of charity she abstained from food eight days, that she might give a poor man the money she would have spent in nourishment during that time. Fourthly, by bestowing upon them things of which she herself stood in need. Her mother having given her thirty-six ells of cloth to make veils and aprons, and other articles of dress, she gave them to two very poor but very virtuous young ladies. Almighty God worked several miracles to enable her to give alms, and He never failed to supply the necessities of the family by extraordinary means when S. Rose, confiding in His providence, boldly gave away what was intended for their support.

One day when she had nothing to give a poor woman, who begged her for the love of God to give her some old clothes, to cover her poor little half-naked children, she took a large cloak, belonging to her mother, and without any permission, beyond that which she interiorly received from God, who inspired her to perform this action, she bestowed it upon her. Her mother being displeased with this sort of liberality, Rose humbly entreated her not to be uneasy, and assured her that Almighty God, who had given her this thought, would make her a return beyond the cost of her cloak. She was not deceived in her expectation, for the same day a stranger came in, and gave her fifty pieces of money; three days after, Dame Mary of Sala sent her, by a servant, a piece of cloth large enough to make another cloak; and the next day the Dominicans gave her several ells of serge, as if they had all combined to return to the mother of our Saint more than her charitable daughter had given to the poor.

Her charity extended still farther; she made herself the attendant and infirmarian of the poor; She took home with her a young orphan lady, named Jane de Bobadilla, of Azevedo, who, besides her great poverty which obliged her to live at the very extremity of the suburbs of the town, had a cancer in her breast, of which no one could bear the insupportable odour. God revealed her condition to S. Rose; immediately she went to see her, offered to wait upon her, and that she might be able to do so, she persuaded her to come to her father's house, where she would render her every sort of assistance; still as she knew that her mother was a little too much attached to her own interests, she told her that she would hire a room in the house for her, and that she would give her the money to pay herself, only requiring that she should keep this a secret. Rose hired the room, brought the lady to it, whom she charitably waited upon, and worked more than usual to obtain the money necessary for the payment of the lodging, which the lady did not quit till she was perfectly recovered.

Her mother having found this out a little later, gave her leave to bring home sick persons, and after this permission Rose exercised her charity indifferently towards the poor women and girls whom she met in the streets, whatever might be their condition. She was not satisfied with giving them a lodging; she nursed them, made their beds, dressed their ulcers,

washed their clothes, and, in a word, rendered them every sort of service, making no distinction between the Spaniard and the Indian, the free and the slave, the European or the African negroes. There was no disease, however loathsome, from which these poor women were suffering, that did not call into action the indefatigable charity of S. Rose, who waited upon them night and day.

When she had no sick persons to attend at home, she went to practice charity at the hospital; and when she perceived anyone whose disease caused her aversion, she devoted herself to her service; and whatever repugnance she might feel, she made her bed, dressed her wounds, fed her, and rendered her the most abject services, although in doing so, she often soiled her habit, which she liked to keep exceedingly clean. She did not practise these virtues without a strong opposition on the part of nature; but she courageously resisted and triumphed over it by the violence she did to her feelings, of which the following is an instance. She went one day to visit a girl in the house of Isabel Mexia, who was very ill, and had been bled two days before. When our Saint saw the green and corrupted blood which had been taken from her, she felt her stomach turn at the sight. Ashamed of this weakness, she asked the servant, who was going to throw the blood away, to give it to her; and taking it with her into another room, she drank it to the last drop, imitating, by this heroic action, her good mistress S. Catherine of Siena, who, having felt the same weakness at the sight of a dreadful cancer, from which a poor woman, whom she had taken upon herself to serve, was suffering, filled a vessel with the matter that proceeded from it, and drank it courageously, to overcome the rebellion of nature.

By her charity she restored a number of sick persons to health; and we might say that the Son of God, to show forth the merit of the mercy she exercised towards them, had communicated to her hands a miraculous power to heal them;

and that, as He formerly imparted such efficacious virtue to the shadow of S. Peter that it restored health, He had renewed this wonder in our Saint, for very often the mere sight of her effected a cure. We will only cite one example, of which the whole people of Lima were witness. Don Juan de Almansa, a man of high rank, being very dangerously ill, desired very much to speak to S. Rose once more before he died: she went to see him, to afford him this satisfaction. When she entered his room, he remarked quite a heavenly beauty on her countenance, from which he conceived a firm hope that she would obtain his cure from Almighty God, Who alone could draw him from the state to which he was reduced. While she was speaking to him he fell asleep with this consoling thought, and awoke in as perfect health as if he had never been ill.

CHAPTER XVII

OF HER CONFIDENCE IN GOD, AND OF THE PROTECTION SHE RECEIVED FROM HIM IN HER NECESSITIES.

A soul which has tasted the goodness of Almighty God cannot be diffident of His mercies, for she knows that He is always disposed to protect and assist her; and the same charity which inflames her will, enlightening her understanding by its brightness, gives her so perfect a knowledge of His Divine attributes, that she finds continually fresh motives for confidence. S. Paul founds it upon three perfections of God, which are, as it were, the agents of His love and His providence, His Power, His Wisdom, and His Goodness.

As S. Rose had often experienced its effects in the loving conduct of God towards her, she had an entire confidence in Him in her spiritual and corporal necessities, and in those of others for whom she solicited graces. She took great pleasure in meditating upon, or in pronouncing these words of the prophet David, "Incline unto my aid, O God; O Lord, make haste to help me." She had them almost constantly in her mouth and in her heart. There were three things in particular, which she was as sure of obtaining as if she had had a revelation from heaven. First, she never doubted of her salvation; secondly, of the inviolable friendship of Almighty God for her: thirdly, of

His all-powerful help in the necessities and dangers in which she might have need of His protection.

She was once seized with a great fear regarding the inscrutable mystery of predestination, which is, in fact, capable of terrifying the most steadfast and virtuous souls. God did not leave her long in this anxiety; He spoke these words of consolation in the interior of her soul: " My child, know that I condemn only those, who by resisting My graces will obstinately lose their souls: continue, therefore, to make a good use of them, live in peace, and be no longer disturbed with this fear." After she received this favourable answer from her Divine Spouse, she had so firm an assurance of her salvation, that when Don Juan de Castille asked her if she had had any revelation, which had given her a certainty of salvation, she confessed to him that Jesus Christ had made known to her that she was predestinated to glory from all eternity; and even when lying on her death-bed, overwhelmed with the pains she suffered in every part of her body, she received an assurance from Heaven that her soul should not pass through the fire of purgatory, and that Almighty God was content, and His divine justice fully satisfied with what she endured from the violent pains of her illness.

In a rapture which she had once in her cell in the garden, she saw in a moment the earth around her all covered with roses. As she was much surprised to see this singular appearance in the season of winter, Jesus Christ appeared to her, and after having caressed her, He commanded her to gather these flowers. She did so, and gave them to Him, but He only asked for one, saying to her, "Thou art this Rose, of which I have a most special care." This chaste spouse understood immediately the meaning of these mysterious words; and was quite consoled to see that God kept it at His right-hand, which is the place reserved for His elect, as a rose chosen from a great number of others. She took the remainder of the

flowers, and made of them a garland, which she respectfully placed on the head of her Divine Spouse, who disappeared after having received it with a gracious countenance, and given her His benediction.

She had the same assurance of persevering in the grace and friendship of God till death, from a revelation by which He made clearly known to her that He had confirmed her in His love, and that she should never be separated from it one moment during her life. In this spirit of confidence she one day told her confessor, that he would sooner make her believe herself to be a stone or a log of wood, than persuade her that Almighty God had a horror or an aversion for her.

This great confidence fortified her mind wonderfully in all the difficulties and dangers which are inseparable from this life, and which so often disturb it. She met some furious bulls in the street without turning out of her way, though her mother and every one rushed into the nearest houses to avoid meeting them, and called to her to run away for fear of being killed; she contented herself with saying, that she was sure these bulls would not hurt her; which was verified on two occasions, to the astonishment of the spectators, who thought her death inevitable.

How great was her confidence in God for things necessary to life! One day seeing that there was no money in the house to buy provisions, nor a bit of bread to eat, she went to open the chest, in the assurance that God, Who never abandons these who trust in Him, would provide for her family. She was not deceived, for she found it full of loaves, whiter and of a different shape from these they were accustomed to eat. On another occasion the honey, which is much used in Peru, having failed, and her brothers having brought word that there was not a single drop remaining, Rose, full of confidence in God, went to the place, and found the vessel quite full of excellent honey, which lasted the family during eight months.

When her father, Gasper Florez, was sick, and oppressed with sorrow at not being able to pay the sum of fifty livres, which he owed, and which he was pressed to return, Rose, being told of it, went to the church to beg God to assist him on the occasion, and not allow him to be put to confusion. As she returned, she saw a stranger enter the house, who gave her father a little purse, containing precisely the sum he wanted to satisfy his creditor. Almighty God favoured Rose's family on many other occasions, and by miraculous means, to reward her admirable confidence in Him, in the great necessities to which her family was often reduced.

Her confidence did not merely regard temporal affairs and necessities; she manifested it particularly in things which related to the glory of God, even so far as to take upon herself, notwithstanding her extreme poverty, to furnish the funds necessary for the Monastery of S. Catherine of Siena, which was going to be erected. She told them that they had nothing to do but to begin to dig the foundations, to collect the materials and seek workmen, and that she would pay for everything; Almighty God had made known to her that her confidence pleased Him, and that He would not abandon her on this occasion. This resolution was spoken of by every one according to their caprice, but nearly all blamed it; some calling it a rash enterprise, others terming it insolence and presumption; even her mother was displeased, and called her foolish and visionary, to talk of raising a building that would cost 10,000 livres and more, when she had not a penny. Rose answered humbly, that God was the guarantee of His own word, and that in a few years she would see this monastery built. Her mother growing more angry, called her silly and extravagant. "Well, mother," answered S. Rose, with her usual mildness, "you will yourself experience the

truth of this prediction, for you will enter this monastery, you will there receive the habit of religion, make your vows, and die in the peace of our Lord." "I become a nun, I!" cried her mother, "what probability is there of that? I am old and poor, and I have never had the least thought of a religious life."

She did not fail, however, to verify her holy daughter's prediction; for in the year 1629, after her husband's death, she received the habit of the Order in this monastery, at the age of sixty. She took the name of Sister Mary of S. Mary, and when her noviceship was completed, she was professed, and died a holy death a few years later. Her poverty was no obstacle to her reception, for she filled one of the places reserved by the foundress for poor girls, who were to be received gratuitously. We shall speak of this monastery in the next chapter.

It will have been remarked from what we have said, that the care taken by S. Rose to assist the poor, and to furnish them abundantly with necessaries in their sickness, was founded only on her generous confidence in God. This was so great, that she took home indiscriminately all sorts of sick women to nurse them, without troubling herself whether or not there was any food for them, or any money to buy the necessary drugs and remedies; she confided so entirely in God, that she never doubted of His coming to her assistance in her charity towards them; and in fact she often remarked, that her family was never better off, or more comfortable, than when she had the greatest number of sick persons to provide for.

CHAPTER XVIII

GOD MAKES KNOWN TO S. ROSE THAT A MONASTERY OF NUNS WILL BE BUILT IN LIMA, UNDER THE NAME OF S. CATHERINE OF SIENA, AND REVEALS TO HER SEVERAL OTHER SECRETS

Love is always communicative; it allows of no secrets between these whose affections it unites; and it is a sort of injustice to give the heart to anyone without revealing all that it contains of any importance. The Son of God Himself gave to His apostles a most incontestable proof of His friendship for them, when He told them that He had made them partakers of all the secrets which He had learned in the bosom of His Father from all eternity. As this Blessed Saviour loved S. Rose so tenderly, and even publicly took her for His spouse, we cannot wonder that He honoured her with the gift of prophecy.

There is in Lima a celebrated monastery of two hundred nuns, of the Order of S. Dominic, built in the year 1622, by the pious liberality of Lucia Guerra de la Daga, an illustrious and very virtuous widow. God had revealed to S. Rose the foundation of this convent ten years before it was begun, and had shown it to her, sometimes by mysterious symbols, sometimes in the same form in which it at present appears, which made her speak of it with as much certainty as if she had seen it built and perfectly finished. She named the persons whom God had chosen to serve Him therein; she mentioned their number; she marked out the spot where it would be built, and sketched the design of it on a table; she told Father Louis of Bilbao, her confessor, that he would be the first to celebrate mass in it; she recognized on seeing her the person whom God had shown her as the first prioress; and transported with joy she went to embrace her, and congratulate her on her election; and by the kiss of peace she gave her, she seemed to consecrate her to that charge for which God had chosen her.

The greater number of these who heard this foundation spoken of so confidently, treated her predictions as the fancies of a heated brain, for there was then no human probability that things would fall out as she said they would. The lady of rank whom she named as the foundress was engaged in the bonds of matrimony, which deprived her of the liberty of disposing of her fortune; she had also several children; and another circumstance which seemed to destroy all hope of accomplishing this foundation was, that the person who had been sent to obtain the permission of his Catholic Majesty for it, had returned without being able to succeed. The prediction of our Saint was, however, accomplished, in all its circumstances; for the lady whom God had chosen to be the foundress soon became a widow by the death of her husband, and a few days after, her five children followed him to the grave, so that she was able to devote her property to this good work.

Almighty God removed the obstacles which the devil's malice and the envy of mankind opposed to this pious design, and so completely changed the minds of several magistrates, whose resistance and obstinacy had seemed invincible, that they not only gave their consent, but became so zealous that they themselves forwarded the execution of the project; and in a short time this famous monastery was built, which still glories in the name of the Convent of the Blessed Rose of S. Mary, though it was not built till five years after her death.

God gave S. Rose the first knowledge of it in a wonderful manner. One day having gathered a quantity of roses in her garden, she began to throw them into the air, quite inflamed with devotion, and giving vent to sighs which the thought of her heavenly Spouse forced from her. Her brother finding her thus employed, and with her eyes bathed in tears, entreated her to tell him the cause of her grief; she would not make known this mystery, but God manifested it to him by the wonders of which he was a witness, for he saw that the roses which his sister had thrown into the air remained suspended there, and having first separated, they reunited, and when all together represented a beautiful cross. He saw also that the roses which she continued to throw formed a border to this mysterious cross. S. Rose knew by divine revelation that these roses represented the great number of holy virgins who would rise above the earth by a generous contempt of its honours, riches, and pleasures, to attach themselves inseparably to the cross of Jesus Christ, by the practice of religious virtues, and the exact observance of the rules and constitutions which were to consecrate these courageous victims to penance.

On another occasion when she was praying, God showed her in spirit a spacious meadow, delightfully enamelled with roses and lilies, enclosed within a garden, which was to be separated from the profane intercourse of seculars. Father John of Villalobos, of the Company of Jesus, a religious of great merit, juridically deposed that he had several times observed in S. Rose a spirit of prophecy, and that she had discovered to him the most hidden secrets of his interior. She showed the same knowledge with regard to Father Philip de Tapia, rector of the college at Callao, and many other persons, whom she admonished of certain things, so secret that they confessed she could only have known them by revelation.

This spirit of prophecy enabled her to see what happened in other places, and she predicted some events long before they came to pass. She assured some persons who were dangerously ill and almost in their agony, that they would recover, though the physicians had given them up, and had remarked in them the prognostics of inevitable death. She foretold to several young men, and to a great number of girls, the state and condition which they would one day embrace; and by this supernatural light she told some that they would enter religion, though at that time they seemed entirely opposed to this manner of life, owing to their engagements in the world. She knew that the viceroy would change his mind, and would excuse Don Gonzalez from the difficult employment which he had destined for him, wishing more to remove him from his court than to do him honour, which change of purpose rejoiced his family, who were inconsolable at the idea of his departure.

She wrote to one of her brothers, telling him that he would have a daughter by his marriage, who would be born with the mark of a red rose on her face, warning him to take great care of her, for she would one day be a great servant of God, and that this supernatural mark was a sure sign of the wonderful progress she would make in charity and other virtues. She knew the deception of a negress, who boldly maintained that she had been baptised at Panama; S. Rose convicted her of falsehood through secret indications, and told her so many secrets regarding her interior, that this poor creature confessed her attempt to deceive, and, powerfully touched by S. Rose's exhortations, demanded baptism. Some difficulty was at first made about granting it, from the fear that she requested it more through human respect than from a true spirit of piety; but S. Rose, who knew the disposition of her soul and that death was threatening her, caused it to be given to her so opportunely, that this new Christian died the next day with every mark of perfect contrition for her sins.

Almighty God, who had enlightened her mind with so great penetration and discernment, that she knew the interior of these who came to visit her, and predicted future events to them, taught her Himself to write, as He taught S. Catherine of Siena. He also made known to her so clearly the time, the place, the day, and the hour of her death, that she spoke of her funeral, and specified particularly what would take place at that happy time.

CHAPTER XIX

OF HER LAST ILLNESS AND DEATH

The same law which obliges us all to enter the world by birth, that we may be capable of being made children of God by the grace of regeneration given to us in holy baptism, requires us to depart out of it by the door of death, in order to take possession of the inheritance of eternal glory, which the Son of God has merited for us by His sufferings, and to which the grace of our adoption gives us a title. This indispensable law of nature makes us regard the death of S. Rose, which filled the town of Lima and nearly all Peru with sighs and tears, in the same light as S. Bernard considered that of S. Malachy, which drew lamentations from all his religious, as the end of his combats, the consummation of his virtues, and his triumphant entrance into heaven.

S. Rose having learned by revelation that she should die on the day which the Church consecrates to honour S. Bartholomew, had from that time a special veneration for this feast, and she passed it in particular exercises of piety; but not considering this sufficient to honour the day, which was to be to her the first of a happy eternity, she caused several little children to fast with her on the eve, and their innocence, being very pleasing to God, greatly increased the merit of this mortification. Her mother was surprised at the extraordinary devotion she had towards this apostle; but she ceased to wonder at it, when her daughter informed her that on this day her nuptials with the Son of God would be consummated in heaven. Having attained her thirty-first year, which she knew by inspiration she should not live to complete, she made the wife of Don Gonzalez, her great benefactor, and the protector of her family, acquainted with the day and place of her death, though she was in perfect health when she gave them this sad intelligence.

The same revelation which informed her of the day of her death, made known to her also the great sufferings she was to endure at the close of her life. Almighty God showed her their number; and told her that her pains would be so violent, that each member of her body would have its own particular torment. She knew that she should have to suffer the same thirst which tormented our Blessed Saviour on the cross, and also a burning heat which would dry up the very marrow in her bones. She did not tremble at the sight of this species of martyrdom; the bitterness of the chalice which God had prepared for her did not shake her constancy; on the contrary, she lifted up her hands and eyes to heaven, to adore the sovereign goodness of her Spouse, Who wished her to partake in His cross and sufferings, that He might communicate to her His glory and His crown. With this generous disposition she entered the Chapel of our Lady of the Holy Rosary, to consecrate her soul and body to the sovereign pleasure of God. Having placed herself on her knees before the altar, she made an act of perfect resignation of herself to the holy will of God, with so great fervour and so tender a sentiment of love and piety, that the fire of charity which inflamed her soul appeared in her countenance; and Don Almansa, who saw this brilliant colour on her cheeks and so joyful an expression in her eyes, thought she must have just received some intimation of her death from her Divine Spouse.

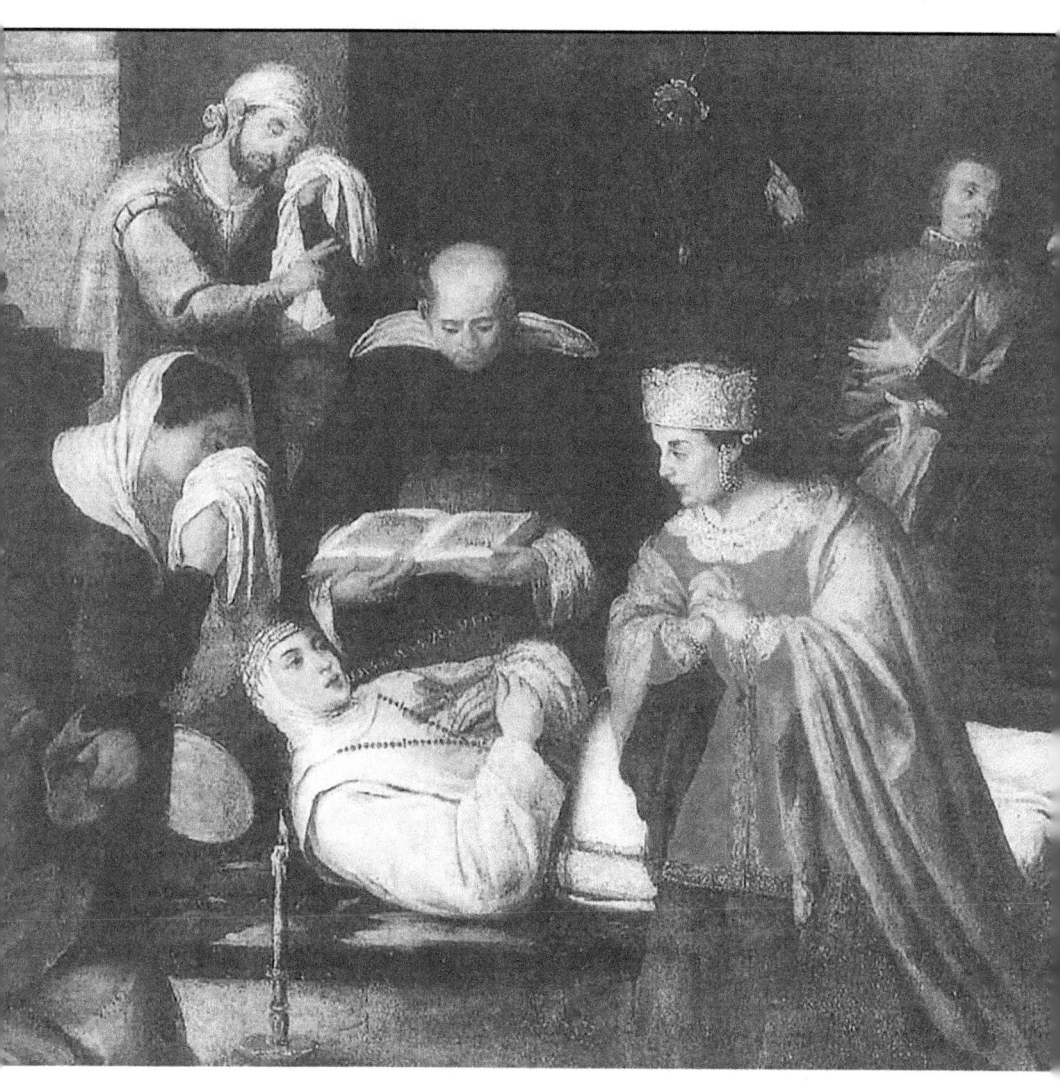

Three days before she was attacked by her last illness, she went to her father's house to bid farewell to her dear hermitage, the witness of the favours she had received from Jesus Christ, the Blessed Virgin, her guardian Angel, and from her dear mistress S. Catherine of Siena: she passed two days therein in acts of thanksgiving, prayers, and tears. In this retreat S. Rose sang, in preparation for death, canticles of praise and benediction to her adorable Spouse, Who called her to His chaste embraces. She then expressed her gratitude to S. Dominic for the care he had taken of her, and for the mercy he had shown in receiving her into his Order amongst the number of his daughters; and after this she entreated, with tears in her eyes, that he would pardon her want of correspondence to her vocation, the infidelities which she had committed in the observance of the constitutions of her Order, and the bad example which she had given to her sisters as well as to seculars. Though the stifled sobs, which her deep sorrow drew from her, choked her utterance, she could not omit to recommend her mother very particularly to him, begging him to be a father to her, and to take her under his protection.

On the first of August she went to her room at night in perfect health, but at midnight she was heard crying and groaning piteously; and the wife of Don Gonzalez, at whose house she lived, having hastened to her with several other persons, found her extended half dead on the floor, cold, without pulse, motionless, and scarcely breathing. In great alarm, they asked her what was the matter with her, and if she did not wish the physician to be sent for to give her some relief. She blushed at this word, " relief," and looking at them with half-closed eyes, she told them in a weak languishing voice, that there was nothing the matter with her, but that she felt death exercising its violence upon her; and as God alone, her sole Physician, knew her state, He alone could withdraw her from it by His power. They placed her again in her poor bed, and immediately they noticed a cold sweat on her face, and so violent a shivering seized her that she breathed with great difficulty; yet she did not cease to pronounce from time to time the sacred Name of Jesus with such tender sentiments and with so much facility, that it was evident that this Divine Name was the only comfort she found in her Sufferings.

The physicians came to visit her in this state, and having diligently examined the opposite maladies, with which she was attacked, they declared that these infirmities and sufferings were beyond human endurance, and that this union of incompatible symptoms was something miraculous: in a word, they were of opinion that her illness was not natural, and that God alone caused it to exist in her weak body, that He might make His destined spouse participate in the sufferings of His Passion.

Her confessor, who did not forsake her in this extremity, fearing that her humility would prevent her from making known the nature and the great number of her sufferings, commanded her, in virtue of obedience, to declare them to the physicians in the best manner she was able, in order to give them at least some slight idea of them. In obedience to this order, she told them that during her life she had been afflicted with every one of the different diseases from which mankind suffer, but that she did not understand that with which she was actually attacked, and that she could not explain to them the pains she endured, except by borrowing comparisons from the most painful sensations in nature. "It seems," she said, "as if a ball of fire were forced into my temples, that it descends to my feet, and that it passes across from my left side to my right, carrying an insupportable heat. I feel," continued she, "as if my heart were lacerated by a burning dagger, and the invisible hand which guides it pierces me sometimes from head to foot, and then, by crossing from side to side, engraves the figure of a cross in my body with this instrument, which burns me with the greatest violence to which fire can attain. I suffer," she added, "such sharp pains in the bowels, that it seems as if each moment they were being torn out with burning pincers; and my head burns as if heated coals, just taken from a flaming furnace, wore placed upon it. In fact, I believe that when I die my bones will be found reduced to ashes, and the marrow dried up, from the effects of the burning heat which I endure."

On this the physicians looked at each other in astonishment at hearing things so extraordinary, and being more and more confirmed in their first opinion by the recital of these dreadful pains, they concluded that her malady was supernatural. Rose, hearing the result of their consultation, ingenuously avowed to her confessor that they were not mistaken in their judgment; and therefore she needed nothing but love and patience to fulfil the designs of God, who wished her to partake in His pains and sufferings. When the physicians had retired, she begged that she might be left alone for some days, and that no one would come to speak to her, that she might be able to converse more at liberty with Jesus Christ her dear Spouse, with whom she felt herself fixed to the cross.

On the sixth day of the same month she ascended with her Beloved, not to Thabor to partake of the glory of His Transfiguration, but to Calvary to bear a part in His excessive sufferings; for on this day her whole left side was attacked by paralysis, and two days after she was seized at the same time with pleurisy, asthma, sciatica, gout, colic, and fever, as if these cruel diseases had united their different pains to make her suffer one which included them all, for she endured inconceivable torments. We may say that this happened by the special dispensation of Providence, who permitted her to be attacked by all these diseases at once, that she might suffer on her bed from the Hands of her Divine Spouse, a martyrdom as meritorious to her, as that which the saints endured on wheels and racks from their executioners.

She preserved always an admirable tranquillity of mind in the midst of her pains; she was so calm in the paroxysms of her fever, in the shooting pains of sciatica, and the sharp attacks of colic, that she appeared insensible, or as if her body were of iron, incapable of pain or change. Though she suffered so much, she never entreated her Divine Spouse to diminish her pains; on the contrary, she begged Him with all the affection of her heart to increase them, in order to punish her rigorously for the crimes of which she believed herself guilty in the sight of His Divine Majesty.

Nevertheless, as the severity of her sufferings brought on fearful paroxysms and convulsions, she began to fear they might cause delirium and loss of reason; she therefore, with tears in her eyes, implored those of her family who were nursing her, to join her in praying God to deliver her from that evil which, above all others, she dreaded. God had compassion on His servant, He was moved by her tears and sighs, and He miraculously preserved her mind sound and entire till her last breath, amidst the burning heat of the fever, which must have caused her to fall into delirium if He had not preserved her from it by His mercy; and, by a further favour, He granted her the use of her tongue, to make known her thoughts till she died. We have the greater reason to believe, that the preservation of her senses was an effect of the Omnipotence of God, as she was often seen during this last illness, as it were, out of herself, without any use of her exterior senses, or in raptures in which her soul seemed to leave her body to unite itself more closely to God.

She suffered from a thirst, which grew more violent every moment, but still she endured it till death without swallowing a drop of water to quench it: preferring to deprive herself of this relief, rather than of the consolation of dying with a burning thirst; and after the example of her Divine Spouse, she asked only for gall and vinegar to drink to increase her suffering.

During her illness she usually confessed her sins every day; and to dispose herself better for death, she made a general confession of her whole life, with such marks of deep contrition, that her sighs and groans were heard in the room adjoining. On the third day before her death she received the Holy Viaticum and Extreme Unction with interior dispositions suited to the excellence of these two sacraments, the graces of which were, in some manner, to put the seal to the merits which she had acquired by the practice of all the virtues.

It was noticed when the Blessed Sacrament was brought to her, that she changed colour, her face became shining and inflamed, and amidst the transports of joy which filled her, she fell into an ecstasy; and after receiving this Bread of angels, which was to fortify her, for the passage from earth to heaven, she remained motionless and totally absorbed in God. In receiving Extreme Unction she disposed her limbs herself, though she had been before quite incapable of moving them, and these around her knew that this holy oil prepared her rather for the glory of her triumph, than for these fearful invisible combats to which the agonizing are exposed; she was indeed assured of her salvation, and Almighty God had revealed to her that her soul, on leaving her body, would go straight to heaven, without passing through the flames of purgatory.

She often declared in an audible voice, that she was a Christian, and desired to die in the faith of the Church, and that she was a daughter of the great S. Dominic. To give proof of this, she kissed her scapular respectfully, and would have it always laid upon her in her sickness. Finally, to imitate the charity of the Son of God, she prayed with all her heart for those who had offended her in word or deed, begging Him

S. Rose of Lima, August 24, 1617

to load them with His graces, and to show them the same mercy which she hoped to experience from His goodness; and holding a little crucifix in her hand, she could not satisfy herself with kissing it, and repeating tenderly, " Father, forgive them."

After having so perfectly copied His love, she had only to imitate His humility before her death; for this purpose she begged that the servants of the house might be sent for, and though she had never disobliged one of them in any manner, she begged their pardon with tears in her eyes. She showed a sensible grief that she had been so great a burden to her mother, and that she should give her yet a great deal of trouble, during the two days she had still to live. She thanked Don Gonzalez very gratefully for his goodness to her, telling him that he would soon be freed from this miserable sinner, who had given so much uneasiness and trouble to his whole family. There was not a person who did not shed tears at these words, and who did not admire the wonderful humility of this spouse of Jesus Christ, who had so profound a contempt for herself, while every one considered her as a Saint.

Don Gonzalez feared that some dispute might arise between the curate of her parish and the religious of S. Dominic, concerning the right of possessing S. Rose's body after death, each having a claim to keep it in their church, the one as his parishioner, for she had died in a house which came under his jurisdiction; the others as their sister, from her being a religious of their Order. To avoid this dispute he thought it would be advisable that she should ask the religious to have the charity to give her burial amongst them, as to one of their sisters, by manner of supplication, rather than by will, for fear that she might become aware of the eagerness which the convent and parish would show to possess her body. She had no difficulty in following this judicious advice, for she knew it was the custom for religious of the third Order of S. Dominic to be buried in the church of his children, and fearing that this favour might be refused to her, owing to the disedification she thought she had given, she begged them with many entreaties to grant her this consolation.

A short time before her death, she was continually in raptures and ecstasies, in which she had a foretaste of the ineffable sweetness she would possess in heaven for all eternity. This violent application of the mind fatigued her weak body very much, and gradually disposed it to die; but her soul acquiring new strength at the approach of the blessed moment which was to unite her for ever to her Spouse, she felt a joy which was perceptible in her eyes and in her words. Two hours before she expired, coming to herself from a long ecstasy, she turned to Father Francis Nieto, and said to him in confidence, "O father, what great things I could tell you of the pleasures and abundant consolations which God will bestow upon His saints for all eternity! I go with inconceivable satisfaction to contemplate the adorable Face of God, whom I have all my life desired to possess."

She then thanked her parents, those who had nursed her in her illness, and particularly Don Gonzalez and his wife, for all the kindness and charity they had shown her. She exhorted their daughters with all the strength that remained to her and with words of fire, to the love of God and the practice of virtue; after this, she spoke privately with her two brothers, and conjured them to lead good lives, and to honour and assist their good mother.

Towards midnight she heard a mysterious noise, which announced to her the coming of her Divine Spouse; she welcomed it with joy; and seeing herself on the point of expiring, she requested her brother to remove the bolster from beneath her head, and to place pieces of wood in its stead. She thanked him for this act of kindness, and placed her head upon them, and as if she had only waited for these pieces of wood, to die upon a sort of cross, she said twice, "Jesus, be with me; Jesus, be with me," and immediately afterwards her pure soul quitted her mortal body, and took its flight into the Bosom of God, to take possession of that heavenly inheritance prepared for it from all eternity. Her death took place on the 24th August, the feast of S. Bartholomew, in the year 1617, her age being thirty-one years and five months.

The same night Aloysia de Serrano had a revelation of her death; and as S. Rose and she had promised one another, that the one who died first would make it known to the other, S. Rose kept her word and informed her of her death and of the happiness she enjoyed.

CHAPTER XX

OF THE HONOUR WHICH SAINT ROSE RECEIVED AFTER DEATH, AND OF THE TRANSLATION OF HER BODY, WHICH TOOK PLACE SOME TIME AFTERWARDS

THE death of the just is attended with circumstances which render it sweet and agreeable: it is not only precious in the sight of God, as their introduction to a throne of which they take possession as conquerors laden with the glorious spoils they have taken from the world, the flesh, and the devil; it is even precious in the sight of men, when they remark on the countenances of the illustrious dead the respect which death pays to their ashes, freeing them from that hideous deformity which gives us a sort of horror even for these persons who were the most beloved by us. The honours which are paid to them after death make us regard it rather as a triumph than as a shameful defeat, and we can scarcely believe that they have paid this indispensable debt of nature, since their virtue makes them live in the esteem of men, while their bodies are lifeless and without motion. In this sense S. Gregory Nazianzen calls the generous Machabees the rivals of a precious death, since they sought it covered with blood and dust in the midst of combats, as a source of life and glory which would render them immortal in the memory of men.

Death appeared so lovely on the countenance of S. Rose, that these who remarked the freshness of her complexion and the redness of her lips, which were separated so as to form a pleasing smile, doubted for a long time whether her soul had quitted her body; for they saw so much brightness in her eyes, and such apparent marks of life, that they could not be satisfied till they had placed a mirror before her mouth, and had perceived that she did not in the least tarnish its lustre by her breath; then they knew that she was dead.

In place of the tears and sighs that would naturally have been expected from the persons who were present at her death, and who had been very dear to her, either by the alliance of blood or by the bands of a close friendship, so great a joy was visible on their countenances, that the house seemed more like the scene of a wedding than a place of tears and mourning.

A person who was present at her death saw a number of angels around her bed during her agony, and she deposed upon oath, that God had revealed to her several days before the death of S. Rose, that her passage from earth to heaven would be glorious and her tomb magnificent; and He had expressly forbidden the use of black drapery, which is a sign of sadness, and desired that they should employ white hangings, as being much more suitable to our Saint's glorious triumph.

In fact, she was placed under ground with as much pomp as would be granted to a heroine, who during life had performed a multitude of great actions; for scarcely had the day-light appeared, before a prodigious crowd of people of all ranks came to the door of the house of Don Gonzalez, in which she had breathed her last; and this surprised the people of the house extremely, for they could not imagine how they had heard of her death, since no one had gone out afterwards. The crowd was so great that it did not merely comprise the heads of families: poor and rich, gentlemen and merchants, priests, religious, seculars, Spaniards, and native Indians entered in confusion and surrounded the body of our Saint. Some kissed her feet with profound sentiments of respect and devotion; others cut off some piece of her dress. They had taken care to close her eyes; but it was impossible to keep them in this position, for they reopened immediately, as if our Saint took pleasure in looking on the inhabitants of Lima, who had had such esteem and veneration for her.

The news of her death having spread itself over the town and neighbourhood, so many people came, that they filled not only the house in which her body was laid out, but the street also; the viceroy was obliged to send soldiers to make a passage through the crowd, in order to carry her to the church, and the multitude was so great in the streets through which they had to pass, that they were several hours without being able to advance.

The Archbishop of Lima, who had quitted his palace to convey the body with his clergy, not being able to reach the house of Don Gonzalez, went to wait for the convoy at the church of the Dominicans, which was about a thousand paces distant. All the religious communities, and all the

Fellow Dominicans carry her to San Domenico

confraternities of the town, came to join in honouring her; and though the chapter of the metropolitan church does not usually attend on these occasions, except for the archbishop's funeral, it was nevertheless present, to increase the splendour of this ceremony. The foreign ambassadors also showed her the same honours as they usually paid only to the viceroys of the country.

The streets through which the body of S. Rose passed on its way to the Convent of S. Dominic were very narrow, and therefore a great number of virtuous and illustrious ladies were obliged to place themselves at windows, that they might have the satisfaction of seeing once more this virginal body, which had been during life the living temple of the Holy Ghost. The poorer people mounted on the roofs to satisfy their pious curiosity; in a word, all the town was present at her funeral, every one wishing to show by this last mark of respect the esteem they had felt for our Saint during her life. The Canons of the Cathedral carried the body a considerable distance, but the eagerness of the principal people in the town to partake in this honour, made them change bearers in every street; the most illustrious amongst the senators succeeded the chapter; after, them the superiors of all the monasteries carried her one after another. Everywhere the people were heard crying out that Rose was a Saint in heaven; and not being satisfied with this vocal testimony, they tried to obtain some portion of her relics, and if the soldiers had not opposed their devotion, they would certainly have cut off all her clothes.

The body being at the church door, certain signs of joy were remarked on her face; and the statue of our Blessed Lady which was in the Chapel of the Rosary sent forth rays of light, which every one took for a miraculous indication of the pleasure she had in again seeing our Saint, who had honoured her with so much love and tenderness. Every one ran to see this prodigy; they observed with astonishment the light which issued from the countenance of this holy image, and there were some who declared that they saw drops of perspiration distilling from it. The Father Prior of the Convent of S. Dominic appointed his senior religious to surround this holy body, as much to prevent the pious thefts of the people, as to bring near the blind, the lame, the deaf and dumb, and a great number of sick people, whom the hope of obtaining a cure through the merits of S. Rose had attracted; and they were not disappointed in their expectation, as we shall shortly see.

The guard of the viceroy and the soldiers of the garrison having made the people retire, they began to prepare for the interment; but so great a tumult was raised, that they were obliged to postpone the ceremony, and unless they had given a promise to the people to delay it, not one would have gone home. This promise having caused these who were in the church to disperse, so great a number of others entered, that the archbishop, seeing that it would be impossible to bury her, made a sign to the religious to carry the corpse into the sacristy; as these fathers thought it was not very safe there they took it away, and placed it in the Chapel of the Novitiate as the most proper place, and the most retired part of the convent, to which seculars have no access. The archbishop being now at liberty to pay his respects to this virtuous servant of God, he placed himself devoutly on his knees before the corpse to kiss her hand, and he found the fingers as pliable and supple as when she was alive.

The next day, as soon as the father sacristan had opened the church doors, and the religious had placed our Saint's body in the nave, an immense crowd of people entered, not only from the town, but even from six or seven leagues' distance from Lima, to be present at her interment. In spite of all the efforts of the soldiers and the viceroy's guard, they could not keep back the people, who all rushed forward violently; some pushed others to enable them to touch this holy body with garments for the sick, with rosaries, prayer-books, or medals: never was there witnessed such a scene of confusion; cripples begged to be allowed to pass that they might be cured by touching her relics; children were lifted from hand to hand over the heads of the people, to kiss her clothes; and with all their precautions, it was not possible to prevent them from cutting her habit, her veil, and her gimp, which were obliged to be changed six times.

The church resounded with the voices of these who were present, imploring her intercession as a Saint reigning with God. The noise was so great, that they were obliged to give a signal to the choir by a bell, whenever it was necessary to answer the Bishop of Guatemala, who was celebrating mass; and it would never have been finished, if the cantors had not left their places to be nearer the altar that they might be able to hear. This illustrious prelate having descended from his throne to approach the coffin, and proceed to the ceremony of interment, was surrounded by a quantity of people, who redoubled their cries and groans; and having given by this means a signal to these who were at a greater distance, that the body of S. Rose was going to be put into the ground, a more numerous troop joined them, and added to the confusion. The religious, fearing some sedition, or that the people would try to seize by force some part of her dress, or of her body, appeased their violent devotion, by making a second promise to defer the burial till the next day.

The people willingly believed this, as there was no appearance of corruption in the body from the heat, for so much beauty was remarked in her countenance, so agreeable an odour was perceived, that everyone believed that Almighty God was renewing in the person of S. Rose the miracle He had so often worked in favour of His saints, by preserving her body from corruption; they thought the body would be exposed for several days to satisfy the people, who were never satiated with seeing her; for during thirty-six hours no

Another view of the crowd and of her Dominican pallbearers

change had appeared in her, either in her complexion or the brightness of her eyes, though the dampness of the place, and the heated breath of the crowds who had filled the church from morning till night, would have been sufficient to effect some alteration in her countenance.

Towards noon the doors of the church were closed, and without waiting for the return of the people, who were troublesome even by their piety, they placed the body of S. Rose in a coffin made of cedar wood, and buried it in the Chapter of the Religious. When the ceremony was completed, the doors were opened to a crowd of people, whose impatience made them furious, and who were ready to break them open with violence. When they saw that they had been deceived, they ran to the grave, and having watered it with their tears, they carried home some of the earth through devotion, to make use of it as a sovereign remedy in their diseases, hoping to be delivered from them by the intercession of this happy Spouse of Jesus Christ. After her death her father's house was every day surrounded by the carriages of the first persons in the city, who wished to see the hermitage which S. Rose had sanctified by her sighs and rigorous penances, and in which she had passed the greatest part of her life, separated from the intercourse of men, but singularly favoured by God.

The frequent miracles which took place in Lima and in the whole kingdom of Peru made her tomb so famous, that the people thought they had not paid sufficient honour to her memory; and it was resolved in the council of state, that a service should be performed for her with greater pomp and magnificence than at first. The archbishop and the viceroy had some little difficulty in fixing the day, that they might both be able to be present; at last they chose the 4th of September, without reflecting that it was consecrated to honour S. Rose of Viterbo in Italy. The people all came to the church on the appointed day, and while the archbishop, the clergy, and the religious communities recommended aloud the soul of S. Rose to God, the people begged her prayers by tears and groans as a great servant of God, the fame of whose sanctity had already spread over all the towns and villages of Peru. The town of Pontozzi, which is about three hundred leagues from Lima, was one of the first to show its respect for the memory of S. Rose, by the ringing of bells, the thunder of artillery, and by placing a great number of lights at the windows. The other towns of Peru vied with each other in showing their confidence in our Saint, by the vows they offered up at her tomb.

The miracles which Almighty God worked there every day to honour her, who during life had immolated herself entirely to His service, drew thither a number of persons from all parts, some to return thanks for the health which they had received from heaven by her intercession, others to implore her suffrages with God to be cured of their infirmities. This fervour never relaxed, as is usually the case with these popular devotions, which begin warmly but insensibly diminish in their progress, till in time they are quite extinguished. On the contrary, it increased so much by the quantity of miracles which were witnessed at her tomb, that all the dignitaries of the city, ecclesiastical or secular, with the principal officers of the council and police, concluded that the body of S. Rose being the precious treasure with which God had enriched the town of Lima, it ought to be made public and withdrawn from the cloister of the religious where it had been buried, to be placed in an honourable position in their church, to satisfy the devotion of the people.

The archbishop joyfully consented; and having given the necessary orders for this august ceremony, he took from the earth the body of S. Rose on the 27th of February, in the year 1619, in the presence of all the religious of the town, of the nobility and the people. As soon as the grave was opened an

agreeable odour issued from it, which appeared miraculous to the numerous assemblage, and they redoubled their joy and respect when they saw this holy body as entire, and the complexion as fresh, as when it was put into the coffin. It was transported from the cloister of the religious into their church, with all the pomp and magnificence that this great servant of God merited, and that could be imagined by the people to show their respect and affection. Father Louis Bilbao, a religious of the Order, a doctor in theology, and a very celebrated preacher, who had long been her confessor, pronounced her panegyric, and extolled with great eloquence the admirable virtues of our Saint. When her *eulogium* was finished she was carried to a little vault on the right side of the high altar; but as the crowd continually hastened thither, as to a second ark, to implore assistance, and persons of all ranks and ages were seen praying there, and offering presents, and leaving their sticks and crutches as glorious trophies of their gratitude for having been cured by her intercession, they were obliged, out of reverence to the adorable Sacrament, to remove these precious relics to the chapel of S. Catherine of Siena, where the people could satisfy their devotion more conveniently, and without fear of irreverence.

In the year 1630, on the 17th of March, an Apostolic Brief was received at Lima, by which the Sacred Congregation of Rites established a tribunal, and allowed the Father Inquisitors to examine canonically into the life, actions, and miracles of the servant of God, Sister Rose of S. Mary, religious of the third Order of S. Dominic. Two years were employed in hearing juridically a hundred and eighty persons, who presented themselves and deposed to what they had seen. Nothing more remained to terminate the proceedings but to visit the relics. They went to her tomb, and having opened it fifteen years after her death, they found her bones entire, covered with dry flesh, which exhaled a delightful odour like that of roses: from thence they went to the Chapter, where she had been at first interred, to see the grave from which the people every day took earth, to which God had communicated virtue to cure fever and other diseases. They found it quite full, with the exception of about five pounds' weight of soil, though several bushels had been carried away during these fifteen years.

In 1640, the Procurator General of the Order of Friars Preachers, hearing of the extraordinary devotion of the people, and the public veneration shown to the relics of this spouse of Jesus Christ, wrote to the fathers of the Convent at Lima, telling them to prevent this exterior honour, for fear of incurring the censures which Pope Urban VIII had fulminated in 1634 against these who should publicly show marks of veneration at the tomb of these who had died in the odour of sanctity, before the Holy See had declared them blessed. In consequence of this order they resolved to prevent the honour which was shown in their church to S. Rose. As soon as this resolution was known in the town, a number of people ran tumultuously to the church, where they loudly complained of this proceeding. And as a rumour was spread that the body of S. Rose had been secretly taken away to be transported from Lima into Spain, the religious were in danger of being murdered, and whatever they could say to the people to undeceive them had no effect, for they were too excited to be capable of hearing their excuses, or understanding their innocence. But their fury having subsided a little, they were told that they had been misinformed; that the body of S. Rose was still in the chapel of S. Catherine of Siena, and that what was done was in obedience to the commands of the Sovereign Pontiff, and that they might proceed to the Beatification of this servant of Jesus Christ in the forms prescribed by the Church, which they must obey, in order to obtain the favour which all the people desired for their fellow-citizen.

CHAPTER XXI

OF THE REVELATIONS WHICH SEVERAL PERSONS HAD OF THE GLORY OF S. ROSE.

There is no saint in heaven, of whom we may not say what S. Bernard said in pronouncing the *eulogium* of S. Victor the martyr, namely, that he instructed us by his example, and employed his credit with Almighty God for our advantage; for the saints were not raised to this eminent sanctity solely for their own perfection, but that the example of their virtues might be an inducement to others to practise the same. And as men cannot imitate their actions, nor call upon them in their necessities, unless they are informed of their happiness, God makes known their merits by extraordinary means, such as revelations and apparitions, that being persuaded of the excellence of their state, they may aspire to their sanctity, and seek to procure by their intercession, grace to attain to it, and relief in their afflictions of soul or body.

By these miraculous means God revealed to many persons the immortal glory of S. Rose, and He made use of her prayers to soften the hearts of a great number of sinners, whose unhappy obstinacy had hitherto given little hopes of their salvation. But before we relate these particular circumstances, we are glad to be able to assure the reader, that nothing is advanced which has not been taken from the authentic examinations which were made of the virtues, graces, and miracles of our Saint. As Aloysia de Serrano, who has been mentioned before, was united with our Saint by an intimate friendship, she was the first to whom God made known the glory which she possessed. One day when she was absorbed in God, she saw the Blessed Virgin before a magnificent throne, holding a rich and bright crown in her hand to place it on the head of some one for whom she seemed to be waiting; on the other side she beheld a multitude of virgins encircling S. Rose, and bringing her joyfully to the feet of the Mother of God. All these illustrious virgins were crowned, and carried palms in their hands; Rose alone was without a crown, and had only a palm; but a moment after she saw the Blessed Virgin place upon her head the brilliant crown she had held in her hand. A person of the greatest experience in mystical theology confessed to Don Gonzalez, his intimate friend, and also gave testimony by words and in writing before the apostolical commissioners, that S. Rose had appeared to him twenty-two times during the three weeks after her death, surrounded with glory.

The physician, Don Juan de Castile, so well known for his virtue,, made oath before the same commissioners, that S. Rose had appeared to him several times, fifteen years after her death, environed with an extraordinary light, and that he saw her in the midst of this light clothed in her habit of religion, but so majestic and glorious that he could not find words to explain her splendour; she held a lily in her right hand, the emblem of her virginity; and during these visions she spoke of the happiness of the saints in so sublime a manner, that he could not express their glory. In the last examination made at Lima, in 1631, he deposed on oath, that for six months, whenever he made his meditation, either by day or night, he had been allowed to see the royal magnificence with which Almighty God rewarded the merits of S. Rose, by means of an angel whom she sent from heaven to invite him to witness this delightful spectacle.

S. Dominic presents S. Rose to the Celestial Court

That which happened to Diego Hyacinth Paceco, a Spaniard, is very wonderful. He was a poor man who earned his bread at Lima by copying writings for lawyers; and Diego Morales, a notary in S. Rose's cause, having pressed him to engross in a very short time, two thousand rolls of writings belonging to the proceedings, and other authentic deeds concerning the examinations which had been made of the life and miracles of S. Rose, he despaired of being able to finish them, on account of the shortness of the time given him, and also partly because his fingers were benumbed with fatigue, and the nerves of his hand entirely relaxed. During the night S. Rose appeared to him; she approached him, and taking his arm she pressed it violently; the pain having awakened him he thought it was a dream; but finding himself perfectly cured he perceived that it was a reality, and that our Saint had truly appeared to him and cured his hand, that he might finish what he had begun in her cause.

She appeared to several other persons after her death, surrounded with odoriferous roses in the delicious garden of her Divine Spouse, particularly to a good widow, who lived at Lima in the odour of sanctity. One day when she was enraptured to see our Saint amidst a great multitude of angels and saints, Rose said to her, "Mother, this state of glory is only acquired by generous efforts; we should work hard, for the recompense with which God crowns our labours is exceedingly great; you see how His mercy rewards abundantly, and even beyond my hopes, the pains I suffered and the few good actions I performed while on earth."

As she was very charitable towards the inhabitants of Lima during her life, she testified to them by several apparitions, that she felt the same interest for them now that she was in heaven; for this widow, when recommending the town to her prayers one day, was ravished into an ecstasy, and in her rapture saw S. Rose, who consoling her said, "Mother, I will do what you ask me, and God has promised to grant me for this dear people whatever regards their salvation; I remember perfectly these things which have been recommended to my intercession, and I will not fail to ask for them."

This is conformable to what sister Catherine of S. Mary testified before the commissioners, to the effect that S. Rose had appeared twice to her after her death. On the first occasion, our Saint encouraged her in the extraordinary pains which tormented her, and in her afflictions; and the second time, she saw S. Rose in the air above her sepulcher, supplicating on her knees the Majesty of God for the town of Lima.

The cure of Father Augustin de Vega, a celebrated religious of the Order of Friars Preachers, and Provincial of the kingdom of Peru, is very remarkable. His life was despaired of, the physicians had given him up, they had ceased to give him remedies for some days, every one being of opinion that his illness was incurable, and that he would never recover. S. Rose appeared, during the night in which his death was expected, to Don Christoforo de Ortega, and desired him to go very early the next morning to the provincial at the convent of his Order in Lima, and to assure him from her that he would recover from this sickness, and that Almighty God had chosen him for a bishop, that he might labour in the service of the Church, and employ the great talents which He had given him. He went, spoke to this dying priest, and making known to him what had happened during the night, delivered the message with which S. Rose had entrusted him: from this time the father began to improve; and some time after he was elected Bishop of Paraguay, and became one of the most celebrated and learned prelates who have governed the Church of Jesus Christ in the New World.

CHAPTER XXII

OF THE MIRACLES WHICH ALMIGHTY GOD WORKED THROUGH THE MERITS OF S. ROSE.

As miracles belong to the number of these gratuitous graces, which God grants rather for the good of others, than for the particular advantage of the person by whom He works them, they are not the essential marks of sanctity; for S. John the Baptist, the greatest among the children of men, never performed any, according to the testimony of Jesus Christ Himself. Still, as they are a subject of astonishment to men, and as they oblige them to acknowledge a Sovereign Power, which has absolute dominion over nature, the Son of God has made use of them to establish religion in every part of the world, and to confirm its excellence and truth; wherefore S. Augustine says, *"semen fidei sunt virtutes."*

We need not then be surprised, if Almighty God has worked so many miracles through S. Rose, a nun of the third Order of S. Dominic, in the New World, where the faith was only just beginning to spring up; for they were necessary to confirm the newly converted, and to strengthen them in the faith. For this reason, though the life of S. Rose was a continual and very famous miracle, God also worked through her means a great number of prodigies, for the salvation of many persons. We do not undertake to relate them all, for the number is so great that a volume might be composed of them; we will content ourselves with noticing the most remarkable.

1.

OF THE CONVERSIONS WHICH THE PRAYERS OF S. ROSE OBTAINED

As the conversion of sinners from crime to innocence, and from sin to grace, is a more noble effect of the charity of the Saints, and a more glorious mark of their power with Almighty God than the restoring diseased and languishing bodies to health, we may say that God has given glorious proofs of the sanctity of His spouse: for a number of hardened sinners, who had been for years in the habit of sin, were struck with compunction and sorrow for having offended God, at the time in which they touched the body of S. Rose, or even beheld it exposed in the church. Father Nicholas de Aguero, of the Order of Friars Preachers, then Vicar General of Peru, testifies in his circular letter of the 1st of September, 1617, that many openly confessed their crimes and disorders, and gave proof by the abundance of their tears and their loud cries, that they were truly converted.

It was remarked, that some young libertines, who came to the church merely to gaze upon the ravishing beauty of this chaste spouse of Jesus Christ, whom they had not been able to look upon attentively during life, returned home penetrated with great contrition, and resolved to change their lives. Some days after S. Rose's death, several persons went to visit Mary Oliva, her mother, and bestowed plentiful alms upon her, in gratitude for the graces which they said they bad received from God through the merits of her holy daughter, who had undoubtedly obtained their conversion from a state of sin in which they had long been.

For several years there had appeared little hope of the

conversion of a man who lived more like an atheist than a Christian, and whose scandalous life was a tissue of all sorts of crimes and disorders; he had never made a good confession in his life, and these who knew his terrible obstinacy looked upon him as lost, for he would not hear anyone speak of doing penance. A pious person, who was sensibly touched by the deplorable loss of a soul for which Jesus Christ had shed His Precious Blood, addressed herself to S. Rose a few days after her death, and entreated her to obtain from God the conversion of this poor soul. Her power with Almighty God was soon manifested; for this man awoke from the lethargy of sin, and the fear of God softening the hardness of his heart, he was converted, and during the rest of his life had as great a horror of sin as he had before had pleasure in committing it. This conversion was much talked of, and greatly augmented the respect which was shown to the merits of S. Rose.

He was not the only person who experienced the favourable effects of her intercession; it is mentioned in the depositions which were taken on the 11th of January, 1617, before the apostolical commissioners, that the number of persons who were converted to God through S. Rose's intercession, and who did penance for their past crimes, was so great in Lima and the whole kingdom of Peru, that a short time after her death so many disciplines, iron chains, hair-shirts, etc. were sold, that the stock of the merchants was exhausted. Father Antonio do la Vega Louysa, the Jesuit, remarks this circumstance particularly; for according to the common opinion of doctors, these conversions are the most certain marks of the sanctity of these who obtain them.

The most infamous public sinners were seen with astonishment to quit their sinful habits and embrace the sweet yoke of chastity, to live for God alone in the practice of rigorous penance, and to apply themselves solely to the important affair of their salvation, seeing in the penitential and crucified life of S. Rose the stringent obligation we are under of attending to it. The priests declared that since S. Rose's entrance into heaven there had been a complete change of manners in Peru, and they knew, by the numerous and remarkable conversions they every day witnessed, that she was powerfully soliciting the salvation of her countrymen. Worldly women renounced their vanity, and left off wearing these rich garments which only serve to nourish pride and ambition, to clothe themselves in the garb of modesty. Religious persons, animated by the example of this innocent penitent, renewed their first fervours so courageously, that nothing was heard in cloisters but the sound of the disciplines, which they took to imitate her mortification. Confessors were besieged in their tribunals by a great number of persons, who testified by their tears and groans the sensible sorrow which they felt for having offended God.

This wonderful change caused a man of rank to give testimony before the Inquisitors, that since the Gospel was preached in Peru by the Dominicans, who were the first missionaries there, no preacher had ever inspired the people with such sentiments of penance, or inflamed them with so great a love of God, as S. Rose had done since her death.

She not only gave her assistance to these who were engaged in sin to withdraw them from it; she also animated very good men to a more perfect and holy manner of life. We may cite as an example Father John of Villalobos, Prefect of the College of the Society of Jesus in Lima, who having visited S. Rose in her last illness, and earnestly entreated her to draw him to the practice of her virtues, felt such interior unction, and received after her death such supernatural lights, as made known to him that she had obtained for him the grace he had solicited.

We may say, in fact, that there was no person, however rebellious to grace and obstinate in sin, whom S. Rose did not induce to enter into himself and rise from his unhappy

. The inhabitants of Lima were greatly scandalized by the aversion which Mary Xuara, the wife of one of the richest and most influential persons in the country, bore towards some cousins of Francis and Alexander de Columa, two brothers who were sons of her husband by his first wife. Francis de Columa took care of these ten little orphans, but his stepmother was not at all moved by their great poverty; on the contrary, she made her will without leaving them anything, and to satisfy her hatred she even did not name them in it. These two brothers being, however, obliged by their business to go into the country and leave these poor orphans at Lima, Francis, touched with compassion at their misery, addressed himself to S. Rose, and looking on her picture he begged her to soften the heart of this obstinate woman, and to inspire her with sentiments of humanity for these little children. The next day this woman, who during eighteen years would not see him, sent for him, and told him that she had passed a miserable night, and that the misery of the ten orphans had been constantly in her thoughts; she begged him to fetch a lawyer to draw up another will in their favour; and this was executed.

Louisa Barba, being almost in her agony, was exhorted by her confessor to have confidence in God, for she would not die of this illness, because S. Rose had made known by revelation that she would be a nun, and would end her life in the cloister. She did not die, but she felt no inclination whatever to embrace this holy state; she had, on the contrary, as great a horror for religion as she would have had for the frightful head of Medusa. Nevertheless, a short time after S. Rose's death, when she went to pray at her tomb, that God would make known to her the state of life for which His Divine Providence destined her, she felt herself so powerfully attracted by Almighty God, that being no longer desirous to resist grace, which had dissipated her unreasonable sentiments, she became a nun of

the third Order of S. Dominic, and was called Sister Louisa of S. Mary.

2.

TWO DEAD PERSONS RAISED TO LIFE, AND MANY MIRACULOUSLY CURED BY TOUCHING THE BODY OF S. ROSE, AND INVOKING HER ASSISTANCE IN THEIR INFIRMITIES

The authenticated miracle of the resurrection of Magdalen de Torrez; which happened in October, 1627, should be placed first on the list, as the most admirable effect of the supernatural power which God communicates to His saints. She was the daughter of a poor labourer, who dwelt in the outskirts of Lima. She was seized with a violent fever and diarrhea, of which she died. She was placed on straw, where she remained from the night she died till the next day: everything was ready for her burial, when her mother, placing her confidence in God and in S. Rose's protection, put on the mouth of her dead daughter a piece of a garment which had belonged to our Saint. Wonderful to relate, this girl, who was quite cold, and whose body had become stiff, opened her eyes, and in the presence of her father and several others who were in her room, rose from the mattress in full vigour and as perfect health as if she had not been ill.

In the year 1631, Anthony Bran, a servant of Madame Jeanne Barette, received a similar favour from heaven through the merits of the same Saint. He had been ill of a fever for three months, and his strength being gradually exhausted, at length he died. These who witnessed his death informed his mistress of it, who seeing him dead, cold, and breathless, lifted up her eyes to heaven, and said, sighing, "God has taken from me this faithful servant, who was so useful to me in my affairs and in the management of my household; may

His holy Name be for ever blessed!" While she was making this act of resignation, she perceived near the dead man's bed a paper picture of S. Rose, and immediately she entreated her protection in her affliction, and earnestly begged her to obtain from God the life of this servant. Full of confidence that she should obtain her request, she placed the picture on the corpse, and while she was on her knees praying with those who were in the room, Anthony came to life, rose up in a sitting position, and published aloud the favour he had received through the intercession of S. Rose, and went the same day to her tomb to thank her.

While the corpse of our Saint was exposed in the church before burial, Elizabeth Durand went thither to touch it, that she might recover the use of her arm, of which she had been long deprived, and which the surgeons pronounced incurable, for none of their remedies could restore its natural heat; but having touched this holy body she returned perfectly cured. A poor slave, a native of Guinea, named Helen, had been tormented for seven years by a quantity of worms, which having exhausted her strength had reduced her to a state in which her life was despaired of. She was attacked by a violent fever, with swellings of the legs and feet, which were sure prognostics of approaching death. Her master, John Merin, being sorry to lose her, hearing of the miracles which were wrought by the intercession of S. Rose, who had been dead three days, persuaded this dying negress to recommend herself to her prayers, and to promise to make a novena at her tomb. She followed his advice: she was carried to the Saint's tomb, and on the last day of the Novena she felt as well as if she had never had this illness.

Beatrice Gavez, who had been afflicted for four years with disease of the chest, from which suffocation was apprehended, having heard of S. Rose's death, slipped with the crowd into the house of Don Gonzalez, in which she had died; and after having recommended herself to her prayers she touched the bier on which her holy body was placed, in the hope of being relieved; from that moment she breathed freely, and her chest was perfectly cured.

The miracle which Almighty God worked in favour of Alphonsus Diaz, through S. Rose's intercession, is not less authentic. He was a poor cripple, well known to every one, who begged his bread from door to door in Lima; he dragged himself along with difficulty on little crutches, on account of a contraction of the nerves, which had some years back so dried up and shortened his feet that he could not support himself on them; as soon as he had offered up his prayers near the coffin of S. Rose, whose assistance he invoked from the bottom of his heart, that he might be cured through her means, he felt his feet stretch out, and having tried his weight upon them to see if he could walk, he found himself perfectly cured.

A negro child, aged twelve years, whose name is not mentioned, and who could only walk with crutches, hearing the miracles spoken of which were worked at the Church of S. Dominic by the merits of S. Rose, crept under the bier on which the body of our Saint was laid and having invoked her assistance, he received so miraculous a cure that he began to run about the church in the presence of a crowd of people, who gave testimony of the miracle. George de Aranda Valdivia, a priest, who had been in the war of Chile against the revolted Indians, and had afterwards embraced the ecclesiastical state, had received in battle several wounds in his left arm, which, not having been well dressed, had caused in the course of time a tumour and inflammation, which prevented him from saying mass, as he could not raise his left arm. Being much afflicted at this circumstance, he went to the cloister of the religious in which the body of S. Rose was to be interred, and having prayed and recommended himself to our Saint, he found himself perfectly cured, and his arm free from swelling and inflammation, and as flexible as the other. Transported with joy, he entered the church, in which were Father Christopher of Azevedo and several seculars, and prostrating himself before the altar of our Lady of the Holy Rosary, he publicly gave thanks to God for the miraculous cure which he had obtained through the merits of S. Rose.

Father Diego de Arasca, Prior of the Convent of Friars Preachers in the town of Panama, having set out for Lima during the great heats, was seized with fever, which reduced him to so deplorable a state, that the physicians seeing his body begin to swell, gave notice to the Father Provincial, Gabriel de Zarata, that the administration of the last Sacraments should not be deferred. The good father received them with exemplary piety, and while the physicians and his brother religious despaired of his life, he recommended himself to S. Rose. His prayer being finished, the swelling and fever disappeared, and the next day he went to the sepulchre of our Saint to return thanks.

Isidora de Montalvo, a very old woman, had been ill for eight months of fever with violent paroxysms, and the physicians thinking her great age rendered her incapable of bearing remedies, had left her. In her extremity she called upon S. Rose, and immediately found herself free from fever. She lived a long time after receiving this favour through her intercession.

There was at Lima a wretched woman, whose name is not given, who hated her husband to such a degree that she poisoned him; and that she might not fail in her design she chose a violent poison, that he might die before assistance could be had. As soon as he had taken the wine with which she had mixed the poison, his body began to swell, a perspiration came over him, and he appeared like a dying person; in the midst of these convulsions he cried out suddenly, "S. Rose, assist me, I promise to make a Novena at your tomb!" His cruel wife, who expected only his death, was terrified at these words, and fearing to be punished for her abominable crime, she stabbed herself with a knife. Her husband recovered at that very hour, and the next day went to begin his Novena, which he finished as an offering of thanks to our Saint.

3.

AFTER S. ROSE'S DEATH MANY SICK PERSONS WERE RESTORED TO HEALTH, AND SEVERAL WOMEN ASSISTED IN THEIR LABOUR, BY TOUCHING HER VEIL, OR SOME PART OF HER DRESS

Elenora Ruiy de Sandoza had long suffered from an almost insupportable pain in the head, which rendered her incapable of mental application. With the design of gaining the jubilee in the metropolitan church at Lima, she put a piece of S. Rose's dress on her head, and was instantly relieved from the pain she had endured for several years.

Another person, named Philippa de Vargas, who suffered from continual fever, felt in its paroxysms a violent pain in her head, as if some one had forced sharp thorns into it; having tried all sorts of remedies in vain, she had recourse to S. Rose, and full of confidence she put a piece of her dress on her head; she fell asleep immediately, and after a pleasant slumber she awoke without fever or headache.

The prioress of the monastery of S. Catherine of Siena at Lima, used the same means to be cured of a severe headache and pain in her chest, which cure she obtained by applying a piece of the dress of S. Rose.

Sister Marina of S. Joseph, a Barefooted Carmelite, had so hurt her eyes by a fall, that she could neither raise nor cast them down; besides this, she suffered continual pain in them. In this affliction she applied a piece of the veil which our Saint had used, and was cured the same day.

Isabel of Mendoza had in her house a little slave girl, three

years old, named Margaret, who had lost the sight of one eye, and the other was so weak that she could scarcely see with it, so that it was thought she would become blind. Her mistress having seen persons in the church of the Friars Preachers thanking God for the health they had miraculously obtained through the merits of S. Rose, thought that her little slave might perhaps recover her sight through her intercession. In this confidence she asked the Father Sacristan for some relic of our Saint, and he gave her a piece of S. Rose's dress. In the evening she placed the relic upon the child's eyes, and having bandaged them she was put to bed. The next morning the skin which had covered her eye was found attached to the bandage on removing it, and both eyes were perfectly cured.

Louisa de Faxado, a widow, who lived at Lima, had lost two of her children, a son aged seventeen, and a daughter ten months old, by epileptic fits; she had only one little boy left, named Francis de Contreras, who was so tormented by the same malady, that he sometimes lay on the ground for fifteen hours in convulsions, foaming at the mouth and struggling, and his mother despaired of his recovery. In this extremity she had recourse to God; and knowing the miracles which He worked through the intercession of S. Rose, she thought she might obtain her son's cure through her merits. When he was one day attacked by a fit of his malady, she placed a piece of our Saint's scapular on his breast: his convulsions ceased at once, he came to himself, and had no return of fits from that time.

The year of our Saint's death, John Rodrignez Samanez, a painter, was troubled with asthma, accompanied by a great oppression of the stomach: this disease had three years before attacked his lungs, and he could only breathe by coughing, or not without a whistling sound that proceeded from his chest. When nothing but his death was expected, Mary de Mesta applied some relics of S. Rose to his stomach; as soon as he had recommended himself to the Saint he fell asleep, and when he awoke found his chest relieved and entirely cured.

A lay brother of our Order, named John Garcias, finding the door of S. Rose's hermitage too narrow to allow him to draw out a footstool, took a knife to cut off part of the wood, but in his eagerness he plunged, the instrument so deeply into his hand that he cut off a large piece of flesh, which hung from his arm in a frightful manner. He had recourse to S. Rose, and taking a piece of her veil he applied it to the wound, and wrapped up the hand in his handkerchief, and an hour afterwards he found his wound as perfectly cured as if it had been dressed by the most skilful surgeons in the country. More than twenty persons witnessed this miracle.

Another still more famous miracle was operated in favour of Blanche de Zuniga, wife of Don Anthony de Contreras, governor of the province of Guilas, in the kingdom of Peru. This lady, who had been eight months with child, being at a country house with her husband, perceived one day that her child no longer moved, and concluded that it must be dead: she remained in this fear five days, and feeling already dangerously ill, she prepared to receive the last Sacraments. While all the family were in the greatest affliction at this twofold misfortune, some pieces of S. Rose's dress were brought from Lima to her husband; as soon as he received them he ran to his wife's chamber, and giving them to her she placed them on her body, and in the space of an Ave Maria, during which time she was occupied in invoking the protection of our Saint, she was delivered of a dead child already putrified and livid, after which she was restored to health.

S. Rose's intercession was particularly available to women, in freeing them from the cruel pangs of child-birth, and preserving their offspring: and for this reason, after her death, a great number of children in Lima had the name of Rose given to them, as a mark of their mothers' gratitude for her assistance in their labour. Nature has sometimes imprinted a mark upon these children, as a glorious testimony of the power which S. Rose had received from God to assist them, of which Peter de Guixano is an example. This child was placed in a cross position in his mother's womb, which by preventing her delivery put them both in evident danger of death in this extremity the mother called upon S. Rose, and when her prayer was finished the infant moved and came easily into the world, with a red rose on the eyelid of the right eye, which nature seemed to have engraved there in memory of this miracle.

4.

SEVERAL PERSONS AFFLICTED WITH DYSENTERY, QUINSY, FEVER, FRENZY, AND OTHER MALADIES, HAVE BEEN MIRACULOUSLY CURED BY EARTH FROM THE SEPULCHRE OF OUR SAINT.

It would seem as if Almighty God had communicated a medicinal and vivifying nature to this earth, in recompense for its having preserved the body of S. Rose from corruption; for the convent of Friars Preachers at Lima being always composed of three hundred religious, they were obliged to procure from Panama a sandy and burning soil, in order to fill up the chapter cemetery, that the bodies being quickly consumed by it there might be room to inter all the religious who died. Extraordinary to relate! that part alone of the ground which received the body of S. Rose changed its quality: it became solid, the earth grew hard as stone, and not being able to scratch it up with their hands to obtain the dust, they were obliged to break it with a hammer, though the rest of the soil in the cemetery was quite light. Almighty God caused this miraculous earth to be, as it were, an inexhaustible source for the relief of the inhabitants of Peru; which was

manifested visibly in 1632, when, after a prodigious quantity had been taken from this sepulchre to be distributed amongst the villages, towns, and provinces of this great kingdom, it did not appear as if more than four pounds' weight had been carried away; for F. Bernardin Marquez, who had been obliged to plunge his arm into the hole, to draw out the great quantity which was sent all over Peru, and even into Spain, perceived with astonishment on taking some out that this earth had increased underneath, and that the space which he had left empty was so completely filled that he could not put his hand into it. This dust worked such miraculous cures that persons came from all parts to fetch it, so much the more eagerly as they witnessed its wonderful effects. We will cite some remarkable examples.

A little girl of six years old had the tonsils of her throat very much swollen by a quinsey; an ulcer had formed; but what made the surgeon fear she would die was that gangrene had commenced in the wound, and the mortified flesh was beginning to fall away in small pieces: they gave her some of this earth mixed with a cooling drink, and the next day she was perfectly cured.

For twenty years the abbess of the Monastery of the Nuns of S. Clare, in Truxillo, had had a swollen leg, which gave her great pain, for there were more than forty ulcers in it, with so much inflammation that she was never without fever: she recovered her health by swallowing some of the earth from S. Rose's tomb, though she had sought it without success for several years in the experience of surgeons and the remedies of medicine.

Sister Grimaneca de Valverde, a nun of the Monastery of S. Clare, lost her sleep so completely with a burning fever and continual loss of blood, that she was fifteen days and nights without closing her eyes, which brought on delirium. The attendants were watching for an interval of reason to give her the last Sacraments and prepare her for death, for the physicians said she had not more than eight hours to live. Isabel of Fuente, the abbess, thought they must have recourse to the mercy of God, and to the merits of S. Rose. In this confidence she went to fetch some of the dust from her sepulchre, and begged the confessor to mix it with water and give it to this dying nun to drink. He did so, she drank it, the fever diminished, the other symptoms disappeared, her senses returned, and after having slept she found herself perfectly well the next day.

Father Ferdinand of Esquivel, sub-prior at Lima in the Convent of S. Mary Magdalen, was troubled with a rupture, which prevented him from preaching or making any journey. One day when he was in affliction at this circumstance, which prevented him from discharging his missionary duties, he was inspired by God to go to the sepulchre of S. Rose. He obeyed the thought, he went to her tomb, and after having prayed that our Saint would assist him in this infirmity, and applied some of the earth, he never felt afterwards any pain, and was so perfectly cured that he resumed the office of preaching which this indisposition had interrupted, and undertook long journeys by sea and land without any inconvenience.

Anne Cortes received the same assistance in a more dangerous and pressing infirmity. After two months of fever she was attacked by pleurisy, which so increased her fever that she became quite purple; she had lost appetite and sleep, and began to prepare for death, which she thought inevitable. Her mother recommended her to S. Rose, and remembering that she had a little of the earth from her grave, she encouraged her daughter to have confidence in the merits of our Saint, and to swallow this earth in some broth; she said some prayers first, and after taking it the purple colour disappeared, the fever left her, she went to sleep and was entirely cured.

Stephen of Cabrera having broken a rib by a fall, felt so much pain from it that he could not sleep; he asked for some of this earth, and having applied it to his side the swelling went down, and he fell into a slumber which relieved his pain; on awaking he found himself perfectly recovered.

In 1618, on the 21st of March, Catherine of Artiaga was attacked in the presence of several ladies of rank by a violent bleeding at the nose, which no remedies seemed capable of stopping, and she prepared for death. A lady having with her some of the earth from S. Rose's grave, put a little into a piece of linen and hung it round Catherine's neck, and immediately the blood ceased to flow, of which several persons were witness.

Father Anthony Montoya, and Father Juan de Estrada, both novices in the Dominican Order, were going to receive holy orders in the town of Guamangan: and as they were passing through a village named Guando, a man, thinking they were two priests, came in terror to request them to go and give absolution to a poor Indian woman who was in her agony, as there was no priest in the village: these two Friars were much grieved that they had not the power of absolving this poor sick woman, and went with the man to exhort her and make the recommendation of her soul. They found her motionless, incapable of speech, and apparently near her end. As they were praying at the foot of her bed, Brother Anthony remembered that he had some of this earth with him, and when the prayers were finished he related to these who were present the miracles which God worked every day by means of it to honour our Saint, and he exhorted them to call upon her for this sick person: he put some in a spoon, and having mixed it with water he made her swallow it. Two hours later these novices being ready to quit the village came again to see her, and on their entrance they found her husband as joyful as he had been sad, and the woman sitting up and eating with a good appetite. When she was told that this earth had cured her she thanked them, and was from that time very devout to S. Rose, and said publicly that she owed her life to her.

The number of these who were cured of fever is so great that it will be sufficient to mention a few names. Joseph do Castro was cured by taking some of the dust in broth. Jane of Mendoza used the same means with success. Father Diego de Palomino, a very learned religious of the Order of Friars Preachers, finding no medicine give him relief in his fever, addressed his prayer to S. Rose, swallowed some of the earth, and was that day cured of his disease. Maria Velasquez, wife of Captain Diego Ruiz de Campos, was freed from a fever and other symptoms which put her life in danger by drinking water with which this dust had been mixed. John of Palomorez was cured of fever and asthma by the same remedy. A short time after, his wife, who had been with child seven months, was attacked by fever, which greatly reduced her; and being unable to use the remedies of medicine, she put her confidence in S. Rose's protection, and took some of the dust from her tomb, which cured her the same day.

We should never finish if we were to try to name all the others; suffice it to say, that with all the care that was taken to keep a list of them, the number of the cured was too great for the pious intention of these who undertook it. John Lobo, a priest, swore solemnly before the Apostolic Commissioners, that he had seen a great number of persons of every rank and age, at Chusco, Potozzi, Orura, and other places of Peru, cured in a moment of their infirmities, and chiefly of fever, after having taken in water a little of the earth from her grave.

5.

PICTURES OF S. ROSE APPLIED TO PERSONS AFFLICTED WITH LEPROSY, QUINSY, GOUT, HEADACHE, AND OTHER

INFIRMITIES, HAVE BEEN THE MEANS OF RESTORING HEALTH TO THEM

The devotion of the people to S. Rose was so great after her death, that there was scarcely a family, not only in Lima, but in all the towns and villages of Peru, that did not possess one of her pictures engraved and printed at Rome, whence they were sent to America. The miracles which God worked through these pictures caused the sick to have recourse to them in their infirmities.

Mary de Vera, the widow of Louis Nunez, had a violent fever with other symptoms, which reduced her to the last extremity, and obliged her to receive the Sacraments in preparation for death, as the physicians assured her she would not survive the next day. She sent, however, to beg Marianne, an Indian woman, who when young had been brought up with S. Rose, to send her a little picture of our Saint which she possessed: as soon as she received it, she kissed it with devotion, and holding it in her hands, she fell into a slumber which lasted till the next morning. On awaking she found herself in perfect health; and full of joy she lighted a wax taper on each side of this picture, and placing herself on her knees she thanked S. Rose for having obtained her health from God for her. This miraculous cure being made known in the town, public thanksgivings were offered to God for it.

In 1631, during the month of December, Mary de los Royes, a little girl of nine years old, was miraculously cured in nearly the same manner. For a year this child had had a disorder in the head which nothing had been able to remove. Her mother took her to the church of S. Dominic, and taking off her cap, touched the picture of S. Rose devoutly with one of her bandages, and hoping to obtain from God her daughter's cure she replaced it on her head; two days afterwards this child was found as perfectly cured as if nothing had been the matter with her.

In the November of the same year a little orphan, ten months old, named Mary, lived with Jerome de Soto Alvarado, who had taken her through charity. This child was so afflicted with leprosy, that she was a horrible object. The servant of the house, seeing that the physicians despaired of curing her, went to pick up in the church of S. Dominic some roses which had been placed on a statue of S. Rose; she took them home, and without mentioning her design she applied them to all the marks of leprosy which appeared on the child's body: having wrapped her up well, she carried her to bed, and found her the next morning cured of her leprosy: in ecstasies of joy she ran to acquaint her master, who hastened to view the miracle, and who went to give testimony of it before the Apostolical Commissioners who were examining the life and miracles of our Saint. This miracle was so well authenticated and so public, that to keep it in mind they ordered that the little girl should be called Mary Rose, which name she bore all her life.

Sebastiana de Vega, the wife of Cyprian de Medina, a doctor of laws and royal advocate, being in the act of mounting a mule to go into the country with her husband, fell when she had her foot in the stirrup, and dislocated a bone, which gave her very great pain, and rendered her incapable of changing her position in bed. One night when she was in great suffering, she desired the servant to bring her a paper picture of S. Rose; she placed it on the dislocated bone with so much confidence, that on awaking from a slumber into which she had fallen while holding this picture, she found herself cured and free from pain.

A poor slave, named Elizabeth Biafora, being very near her confinement, was seized with pleurisy, violent fever, and vomiting; the physicians seeing these symptoms in a person who was not in a state to use their remedies, caused her to receive the last Sacraments, thinking she could not recover. This poor woman seeing there was no human hope, put all her confidence in God; she earnestly asked for a picture of S. Rose, which she applied to the side in which she felt pain, and left it there all night. The next morning the physicians

being come to try to save at least the child's life, were much surprised to find her in perfect health and asking for something to eat. The day after this miracle her confinement took place happily, and she was able to nurse the child herself.

In 1632 Angelica de Albido, wife of Francis de las Cuentas, who was with child of twins, was delivered of one, but the other still remained, and the matrons who attended her thought she would die. Her husband was inconsolable; and in this consternation the sick person had recourse to S. Rose, and asking for one of her pictures, she had it fixed to the foot of her bed, that it might be always before her eyes. While she was heartily praying to her to help her in this extremity, she felt pains come on, and in the same moment a second daughter came into the world. In memory of this miracle they were named in baptism Mary and Frances de Rose. The history of her life from which these miracles have been taken relates twelve more which are well authenticated, and which were wrought by the application of her pictures.

CHAPTER XXIII

OF THE EFFORTS MADE AT ROME TO OBTAIN FROM THE POPE HER CANONIZATION.

As honour is the reward of virtue, it has always in every country been rendered to illustrious men who have signalized themselves by glorious actions, or who have well served the people or the state; and as in the idea of pagans apotheosis constituted the height of glory, supreme honours have been offered to these emperors and heroes who had made themselves renowned by the mildness of their government, or by the splendour of their triumph. The Christian religion, more enlightened in the discernment of the honour she pays, and more just in the recompense which she awards to virtue, consecrates the more solid and the more noble rewards to these who have perfectly imitated the Son of God by the exact practice of the heroic virtues which He preached on earth by word and example; she praises their merit, she pronounces panegyrics in their honour, and to render them immortal in the memory of man she grants them the honour of a sacred apotheosis, declaring to the people that they are reigning with God, and that they may offer to them public testimonies of honour and respect. The eminent virtue of S. Rose, sustained by such great and continual miracles, rendered her so faithful a copy of the virtues of Jesus Christ, that we may say in her praise what Hildebert said of a lady who was very pious and closely united to God, "*In ea praeter virtutem, nihil virtus invenit.*"

We need not be astonished that after her death the kingdom of Peru most earnestly solicited the honours of canonization for her from the Holy See. The metropolitan church of Lima, all the religious Orders of S. Francis, S. Augustine, the Carmelites, the Order of Mercy, of S. John of God, and Father Nicholas Mastrillo, Provincial of the Society of Jesus, in the name of the whole Society, wrote letters to the Pope, in which they very humbly entreated His Holiness to proceed to the canonization of the admirable servant of God, Sister Rose of S. Mary, whom the people honoured for her virtues, and whose miracles rendered her illustrious throughout the New World. The viceroy, the council of state, the governors of the province, and the magistrates of the towns, united for the same end, and joining their solicitations to these of the prelates, the clergy, and all the religious communities, entreated not only for her canonization, but that S. Rose might also be given as Patroness to Lima, the capital of the kingdom of Peru. A brief was dispatched from Rome, by which His Holiness appointed Apostolic Commissioners to examine on the spot her life, her conduct, and the miracles wrought at her tomb. It was thought that the depositions of a hundred and eighty-three witnesses would soon enable them to see the desires of all Christian America satisfied; for on the 22nd of March, in 1625, Cardinal Peretti, Prefect of the Congregation of Rites, having examined the depositions which had been juridically taken at Lima of the life and miracles of S. Rose, issued a decree in which he declared that His Holiness might cause information to be taken by apostolic authority.

On the appearance of this decree Pope Urban VIII sent a Brief to the Archbishop of Lima, and in his absence to the Bishop of Guatemala, giving him for coadjutors the dean and the archdeacon of the church of Lima. They were so diligent, that the proceedings were finished and presented to the Congregation of Rites on the 22nd of July, 1634. Cardinal Torrez, who had succeeded Cardinal Peretti, acknowledged their authenticity; but a Brief which His Holiness published the year following, prohibiting new devotions, stopped the whole affair. After the death of Urban VIII, the solicitations were continued under Innocent X, but delays were caused by unavoidable circumstances.

Urban VIII

Under Alexander VII the petition was renewed, and Father Anthony Gonzalez, Definitor of Peru, and Procurator in this affair, was so active in the business, that on the 13th of September, 1663, Cardinal Azzolini having made a discourse in the Congregation of Rites before His Holiness on the heroic virtues of S. Rose, and also on the miracles which God daily worked through her merits, it was resolved to proceed to her canonization. Father Gonzalez repeated the solicitations which had been made to three preceding Popes, in the name of the clergy, the nobility, and the people of Peru. He presented to the Pope the requests of nine religious Orders, three letters from the King of Spain, and three from the Cardinal of Arragon, on the same subject.

The Very Reverend Father John Baptist de Marinis, of the Order of Friars Preachers, presented to him two requests in the name of his whole Order, by which he made known to His Holiness the persevering devotion of all Peru, in honouring the Venerable Sister Rose of S. Mary as a Saint, whose merits it had pleased God to exalt by a hundred and nineteen new miracles; but the war with the Turks in Hungary,

Alexeander VII

and other affairs, caused the decree to be delayed a little longer: Divine Providence had reserved the glory of the accomplishment of the proceedings to our Holy Father Pope Clement IX. The Queen-Regent of Spain pressed the matter so earnestly that His Holiness commanded the Congregation of Rites to assemble for this purpose. After several meetings their decree was published on the 10th of December, 1667, by which they declared that His Holiness might proceed to the canonization of this servant of God, and might permit her in the meantime to be honoured under the name of Blessed.

Clement IX

The Brief of Clement IX for the beatification of S. Rose is dated the 12th of February, 1668; and she was canonized three years later, 1671, by Clement X., who appointed the 30th of August for her feast. Thus solemnly has the Church of God set the seal of her unerring approval upon that series of wonders, that endless chain of miracles, which, reaching from her cradle to her grave, make up the life of this American virgin.

There was never a time and never a land when and where it was more needful for the daughters of the Church to learn how to make for themselves a cloister in the world than England in the present age; and it is precisely this lesson which the Life of S. Rose conveys. Amidst so much that is false and hollow, heartless and unreal, how beautiful before Almighty God, would be the childlike simplicity of this virgin of the South, copied even faintly in the lives of our Catholic countrywomen!

Clement X

For it is this simplicity which was her fairest ornament; indeed, so completely child-like was she herself, and so child-like the wonders with which her Divine Spouse encircled her, that in reading her Life it seems hardly ever to strike us that she was anything but a little girl. It is as though she grew no older, but remained still the baby, cradled in the arms of Jesus, as when the vermilion rose bloomed miraculously on her little face when three months old. Let us also thank Almighty God in the

1586 - 1617

fervent simplicity of our faith for the seal His Church has set upon these authentic wonders; wonders not lost in dubious antiquity, but adequately proved in the face of modern criticism so short a time ago; and remembering that this bold exhibition of the marvellous is by no less an authority than the Catholic Church presented to our veneration and our love, let us take it like awestruck children, as a page from the lost chronicles of Eden, and strive to unlearn that bold timidity with which we have too often been inclined to court favour where we shall never get it, and to avoid sneers which are to us as an heritage and vouchers of our truths, by smiling with the profane and doubting with the sceptical. For one of the faithful to try to look as like an unbeliever as he can is a sight which never won a soul to Christ, or gained for the Church the esteem of an opponent. Rose of Lima is now raised upon the altars of the Church by the decree of her canonization; she is a Catholic Saint: no sneer of man can wither the marvellous blooming of her leaves; but he will find a thorn who shall dare to handle roughly this sweet mysterious Rose which S. Dominic planted in the garden of his Master.

F.W. Faber.

*In religious life
a man lives more purely.
Falls more rarely.
Rises more promptly,
Walks more circumspectly,
Receives the waters of grace
more frequently
Reposes more securely,
Dies more confidently,
Is cleansed from his faults
more quickly,
And in Heaven receives
a more magnificent reward.*
—St. Bernard of Clairvaux

Saints Rose, Martin and Turibius

IMAGE INDEX

In the image citations for *The Life of St. Rose* by Feuillet the Arca listing refers to "Arte Colonial Americano- Universidad de los Andes. Proyeto ARCA Cultura visual de las Americas http://artecolonialamericano.az.uniandes.edu.co:8080/." Searching "Santa Rosa de Lima" on that site will bring up 280 images of S. Rose which is a large proportion but by no means all of the art which her life inspired in the 17th and 18th c. She evidently had as great an impact on that era as S. Therese on ours. She is patroness of the Americas, and one could fairly say, too, our S. Catherine of Siena.

Page II. St Catherine of Siena, "According to Augusta Drane, in *The History of St. Catherine of Siena and Her Companions* (1899), vol. 1, p. 184: "'Two likenesses exist of St. Catherine of Siena: one is the celebrated painting by Andrea di Vanni . . . the other is the almost equally celebrated marble bust which claims to be the work of Jacobo della Quercia, and to have been carved by him from a cast taken after her death.' The bust is on display in the church of San Domenico, Siena. (photo by Fra Mario Di Marco, OP)" http://50.63.119.146/Bust.htm

Page XIII. La Merced. Michael A. Fuentes, *Lima, Sketches of the Capital of Peru* (Paris: Firmin, 1866). The church and convent of La Merced were built in 1534 by Hernando Pizarro, brother to the Conqueror, and cost 700,000 piastres. The church has twenty-three altars." Fuentes, *Sketches,*24. The other churches of Lima were similarly furnished with many altars, no doubt to accomodate the private Masses of the many priests who resided n Lima. S. Rose frequented these and other churches of the city.

Page XIV. Dominican shield: in Domingo Augulo, O. P., del Instituto histórico del Peru. *Santa Rosa de Santa Maria, Estudio bibliográfico* (Lima: Sanmarti y cia, 1917), title page.

Page XIX. Harquebusier."The harquebusier was the most common form of cavalry found throughout Western Europe during the early and mid 17th century. Early harquebusiers were characterised by

IMAGE INDEX

the use of a form of carbine, called a "harquebus." Image and text from Wikipedia.

Page XXI. Decorative title page: Fuentes, *Lima,*

Page XXII. Nacimiento de la Santa Rosa de Lima, Basilio Pacheco, Actividad1738 - 1752

Page 3. The Baptism of St. Rose. The ARCA listing: "Bautizo de Santa Rosa de LimaAnónimo, Fecha: 1700-1799"; http://52.183.37.55/artworks/2654

Page 6. Cathedral, Fuentes, *Sketches,* 16.

Page 13. Church of San Sebastian. "Built in 1544, its construction is attributed to Francisco Becerra, was the first parish of Lima, and here saints and illustrious Peruvians were baptized as was Santa Rosa de Lima, San Martin de Porres, José Santos Chocano. Francisco Bolognesi, among others. "_(https://www.go2peru.com/peru_guide/lima/religious_monuments.htm) The photo is from https://jpelsous.tumblr.com/post/168044205413/iglesia-parroquial-de-san-basti%C3%A1n-ss.

Page 15. St. Rose refuses a suitor: ARCA listing: "Santa Rosa de Lima rechaza un pretendiente; Anónimo, Fecha: 1700-1799."http://artecolonialamericano.az.uniandes.edu.co:8080/artworks/7540.

Page 17. S. Turibius, Wikimedia Commons.

Page 19. St. Rose takes the habit: ARCA listing: "Serie de la Vida de Santa Rosa de Lima, S. Rosa toma el hábito de terciaria; Anónimo, Fecha: 1600-1699."

Page 20. Dominic in Penitence, by Luis Tristán c. 1610-1624: Santo Domingo penitente https://commons.wikimedia.org/wiki/File:Luis_Trist%C3%A1n_-_St_Dominic_in_Penitence_-_Google_Art_Project.jpg.

Page 24. Church of St. Augustine, Fuentes, Sketches, 24. Fuentes writes: "San Agustin. — This church was built in 1554. Archbishop Loaiza laid the first stone, and the whole of the cost was defrayed by Hernan Gonzales de la Torre and his wife Donna Juana Cepeda. The church has sixteen altars."

Page 26. An indian woman. Fuentes, Sketches, ,202.

Page 28. S. Rose Takes the Discipline: "Santa Rosa en actitud penitente" in Carlos Page, "La vida de Santa Rosa de Lima en los lienzos del convento de Santa Catalina de Córdoba (Argentina)." https://www.academia.edu/22876718/La_vida_de_Santa_Rosa_de_Lima_en_los_lienzos_del_convento_de_Santa_Catalina_de_C%C3%B3rdoba_Argentina.

Page 31. Indian with bundles, *Sketches,* 95.

Page 33. Apotheosis of St. Rose.

Page 35. Horse drawn carriage, *Sketches, 150*

Page 36. Bridge over the Rimac, the river that divides Lima. Fuentes, *Sketches*, 10.

Page 39. Indian woman with baby, Fuentes, *Sketches*, 172.

Page 40. St. Rose sewing; ARCA lisitng: "Santa Rosa de Lima bordando; Anónimo,Fecha: 1700-1799." http://52.183.37.55/artworks/7824.

Page 43. A pescadora (fish monger), Fuentes, *Sketches*, 155.

Page 45. Rose with hair nailed to wall: *"Santa Rosa de Lima penitente*; Autoría desconocida." http://artecolonialamericano.az.uniandes.edu.co:8080/artworks/2656.

Page 47. Map of Lima: Carolina Salazar Marulanda, *Plaza Fundacional En El Siglo xx* (Bogotá, Colombia: Universidad Nacional de Colombia, 2012), 177.

Page 51. S. Rose 's friendship with mosquitos: Page, *La Vida*. "La amistad de Santa Rosa con los mosquitos. Monasterio de Santa Catalina de Siena en Córdoba, Argentina" in Carlos Page, *La Vida*.

Page 52. *The Espousal*: Nicolás Correa (ca. 1660 - ca. 1720) - The Mystic Betrothal of Saint Rose of Lima. https://commons.wikimedia.org/wiki/File:Nicol%C3%A1s_Correa_-_The_Mystic_Betrothal_of_Saint_Rose_of_Lima_-_Google_Art_Project.jpg

Page 54. St. Rose's Vision of Paradise: ARCA listing: "Vision del paraiso de Santa Rosa de Lima, Anonimo, Fecha 1700-1799; artecolonialamericano.az.uniandes.edu.co:8080/artworks/2640"

Page 56. Dominican Tryptch by Gregorio De Ferrari, with S. Rose, S. Vincent Ferrer, and S. Louis Beltran, in the Convento di San Domenico (Taggia). Foto by Carlo Dell'Orto at https://commons.wikimedia.org/wiki/File:Gregorio_de_ferrari,_i_ss._rosa_da_lima,_vincenzo_ferrer_e_luigi_bertr%C3%A0n,_San_Domenico_(Taggia).jpg.

Page 58. A Franciscan. Fuentes, *Sketches*, p. 26.

Page 63. The Virgin with S. Rose and S. Dominic: La vierge avec l'enfant remettant un rosaire à saint Dominique en présence de saint Rose de Lima, patronne des Amériques by Onorio Marinari. https://commons.wikimedia.org/wiki/File:Onorio_Marinari_La_Vierge_avec_l%27Enfant.jpg

Page 64. S. Rose collects water from a fountain; Santa Rosa recoge agua de una fuente. Monasterio de Santa Catalina de Siena en Córdoba, Argentina in Carlos Page, "La Vida."

Page 69. Rose before the Inquisitors; ARCA listing: Santa Rosa de

IMAGE INDEX

Lima ante los inquisidores. Laureano Dávila, Fecha: 1700-1799, http://52.183.37.55/artworks/388

Page 70. A nun. Fuentes, *Sketches*, p. 31.

Page 72. Noble lady. Fuentes, Sketches, 103

Page 75. S. Rose drinks from the side of Christ: Cristo le da de beber a Rosa sangre de su costado abierto. Lienzo de Cristóbal de Villalpando en el retablo de Santa Rosa de Lima, ca. 1702. Parroquia de los Santos Apóstoles Felipe y Santiago, Azcapotzalco, Ciudad de México. http://books.openedition.org/cemca/docannexe/image/2318/img-8.jpg

Page 79. S. Rose with infant by Bartolomé Esteban Murillo 1617-1682. https://www.wikiart.org/en/bartolome-esteban-murillo/st-rose-of-lima

Page 82. S. Catherine of Siena; Robert Staes, O.P. http://www.domcentral.org/library/BobStaes/index.html

Page 85. Figure from Fuentes, *Sketches*

Page 88. Holy card.

Page 91. Lady cooking, "Indian picantera": Fuentes, *Sketches,* 126.

Page 92. A mansion in Lima, Fuentes, *Sketches*, 9.

Page 95. Woman on horse, Sketches, 151.

Page 97. ARCA listing: Serie de la Vida de Santa Rosa de Lima, S. Rosa envía un ángel de la guarda; Anónimo, Fecha: 1600-1699.

Page 99. ARCA listing: Defensa de la Eucaristía con Santa Rosa de Lima, 01 Anónimo,Fecha: 1650-1699

Page 104. A priest. Fuentes, *Sketches,* 32.

Page 106. ARCA listing: Bodas místicas de Santa Rosa de Lima, Juan-Tinoco, Fecha: 1680

Page 111. The Viceroy.Luis de Velasco, 1st Marquess of Salinas (known as Luis de Velasco, hijo to distinguish him from his father) (c. 1534, Carrión de los Condes, Spain – September 7, 1617, Seville), was a Spanish nobleman, son of the second viceroy of New Spain, and himself the eighth viceroy. He governed from January 27, 1590 to November 4, 1595, and again from July 2, 1607, to June 10, 1611. In between he was viceroy of Peru for eight years (July 24, 1596, to January 18, 1604).

Page 112. S. Catherine:"The famous fresco of Catherine of Siena by Andrea di Vanni, one of her many disciples. Vanni, besides being a well-known painter, was also a politician. According to tradition, he painted the fresco on one of the pillars in the Capella delle Volte ("Chapel of the Veils"), where Catherine and the other Mantellate

prayed in
the church of San Domenico in Siena. Later, the fresco was placed above the altar in the same chapel where it can be seen today." From www.drawnbylove.com http://www.drawnbylove.com/Vanni%20portrait%20of%20Catherine.htm

Page 114. Bunuelera (fritter-woman). Fuentes, *Sketches*,

Page 115. Indian woman with pots, Fuentes, *Sketches*, 199

Page 116. Woman with vase. Fuentes, *Sketches*,198

Page 117. Mulatress, Fuentes, Sketches, 81

Page 118. Servant woman praying, Fuentes, *Sketches*, 78

Page 119. Indian woman with braided hair, Fuentes, *Sketches*, 92

Page 122. S. Rose as nurse; ARCA listing: Santa Rosa de Lima enfermera, Anónimo, Fecha: 1700-1799.

Page 124. Misturera (flower-girl) of the Arcades. Fuentes, *Sketches*, 219.

Page 127. Saint Rose of Lima praying in the Hermitage: ARCA listing: Santa Rosa de Lima rezando en la Ermita, Francisco Martínez, Fecha: 1740-1770.

Page 129. Melon hawker of Lima. Fuentes, *Sketches*,201.

Page 130. Kneeling nun, Fuentes, *Sketches*, 33.

Page 133. S. Rose with noble lady in garden: ARCA listing: Los árboles se inclinan ante Santa Rosa de Lima, Laureano Dávila, Fecha: 1700-1799. http://52.183.37.55/artworks/386.

Page 135. A nun. Fuentes, Sketches, 34.

Page 136. The Acho Promenade, Fuentes, Sketches, 71.

Page 139. Death bed scene: Muerte de Santa Rosa de Lima. Lienzo atribuido a Angelino Medoro. Basílica Santuario de Santa Rosa, Lima.http://books.openedition.org/cemca/docannexe/image/2318/img-14.jpg.

Page 145. "Retrato auténtico de Sta Rosa de Lima, original de Angellno Medoro.—1617. (Santuario de Sta. Rosa)" in Augulo, *Estudio*, 11. Given that S. Rose died in 1617, that her eyes are closed, and that she would have been resistant to portaits, presumably this portrait was done post-mortem.Page 148. Sculpture: Tránsito de Santa Rosa. Escultura en mármol de Melchor Caffá, 1665. Iglesia de Santo Domingo, Lima. http://books.openedition.org/cemca/docannexe/image/2318/img-17.jpg.

Page 151. Dominicans carry her body; ARCA listing: Serie de la Vida de Santa Rosa de Lima, Funerales de S. Rosa, Anónimo, Fecha: 1600-1699. http://artecolonialamericano.az.uniandes.edu.co:8080/artworks/4694.

IMAGE INDEX

Page 155. Entierro de Rosa. Grabado de Cornelis Galle. En Juan del Valle, Vita et historia S. Rosae As. Maria, Amberes, primera mitad del s. xvii.http://books.openedition.org/cemca/docannexe/image/2318/img-15.jpg.

Page 158. Rose gazing upward at infant. Claudio Coello (1642–1693).

Page 161. French holy card.

Page 164. ARCA listing: Santo Domingo por intermedio de la Virgen presenta a Santa Rosa de Lima ante la corte celestial, Angelino Medoro, Fecha: 1700-1799 http://52.183.37.55/artworks/2643.

Page 172. Rose of Lima and Pope Pius V by Giovanni Ceffi - Mazzoleni Altar - Sant'Anastasia - Verona.

Page 178. ARCA listing: Santa Rosa de Lima coronada por el niño Jesús, Gregorio Vásquez de Arce y Ceballos, Fecha: 1650-1700. http://artecolonialamericano.az.uniandes.edu.co:8080/artworks/16156.

Page 182. ARCA listing: Santa Rosa de Lima y el milagro de los claveles, Anónimo, Fecha: 1700-1799. http://artecolonialamericano.az.uniandes.edu.co:8080/artworks/7658.

Page 189. S. Rose holy card.

Page 191. S. Rose holy card.

Page 194-195. Popes from Wikipedia.

Page 196. Holy card with dates.

Page 197. "Fin," Fuentes, *Sketches*, 220.

Page 234. painting.

Have we Catholics of the 21st century lost contact with the glories of our past? It seems undeniable. Arthur M. Gilbert and Son is dedicated to re-discovering, re-typesetting, and re-issuing classic and simply inspiring books in an affordable and beautiful format. So much saintly literature and lives of the saints are in fact in print, but machine read, speed copied and priced outrageously. We, on the other hand, are producing high quality books, copiously illustrated and eminently affordable.

ARTHUR M. GILBERT AND SON, PUBLISHERS
MILWAUKIE, OREGON

THE REAL DE RANCÉ

ILLUSTRIOUS PENITENT AND REFORMER OF NOTRE DAME DE LA TRAPPE

AILBE LUDDY

Penitent Extraordinaire

Armand Jean de Rancè was a penitent priest. He became, incredibly, the saintly founder of the Trappists in late 17th c. France. His strict interpretation of the Rule of St. Benedict re-invigorated the Cistercian order of his day, an order which in its time had been salt and light for all of Christendom. Founded in 1098, within decades the Cistercian order had populated all of Europe with hundreds of fervent monasteries, but by Rance's time had fallen into mediocrity and disorder. While his reforms restored his abbey and attracted ardent candidates from all over France, his interpretation of the Rule of St. Benedict was very controversial in his time and in ours as well. By now practically all that the Cistercians keep of the Trappist charism is the name, and both de Rancè and his writings are hardly known among them.

Surely this is due in part to the odium that Henri Bremond, S.J. poured on him in his book *Tempetè* (published as *The Thundering Abbot* by Sheed and Ward in 1930). In *The Real de Rancè* Fr. Ailbe Luddy, a Trappist of Mount Melleray Abbey in Cappoquin, Ireland, responds to Bremond and thoroughly rehabilitates the reputation of this saintly abbot.

Order on Amazon!

Again we have RANCÉ in print:

DE LA SAINTETÉ ET DES DEVOIRS DE LA VIE MONASTIQUE

by the **Abbé Armand-Jean de Rancé** was translated and titled

ON THE SANCTITY AND THE DUTIES OF THE MONASTIC STATE

by Dom Vincent Ryan of Mount Melleray Abbey in **1830**.

Now As

BACK TO ACETICISM: THE TRAPPIST OPTION

An edition of 650 pages in two volumes, Dom Ryan's translation, has been **re-typeset, re-titled, edited, updated, annotated, and its many citations corrected and amplified.** Also, we have supplied it with **52 illustrations** together with an **Image Index** and an **Index of Scriptural Citations.**

To foster its wide circulation and **the speedy recovery of monasticism** it is **currently** available to you on **Amazon** at **far less cost** than comparable books.

Back to Asceticism: The Trappist Option

A Translation with Introduction and Notes of
DE LA SAINTETÉ ET DES DEVOIRS DE LA VIE MONASTIQUE

Armand-Jean de Rancé

Praise for Rancé's *De la Saintete*

"His *De la Saintete* is unquestionably one of the most important works of post-medieval Cistercian writing and occupies a major place in the history of spirituality."

DAVID N. BELL, author of *Everyday Life at La Trappe Under Armand-Jean Rancé, Understanding Rancé*

"This work, treating of the sanctity and the duties of the monastic life, contains a doctrine accurately derived from Holy Scripture and the tradition of saints. The reading of it will discover to monks the obligations and the perfection of the angelic state to which they have been called. It will prove not less profitable to people in the world by making them understand, from the austerities and the humiliations practiced in the cloister, how great is the corruption in which we live, how deeply the poison has penetrated our hearts, and how violent and incessant must be our efforts against ourselves if we hope not merely to prevent the growth of vicious habits but to pluck them up by the roots."

JACQUES-BÉNIGNE LIGNEL BOSSUET, Bishop of Meaux (1681-1704

It used to be said formerly that one should have lived like St. John Climachus so as to be able to compose his divine *Ladder of Perfection*. The same can be said of the author of this book. Five years ago I had the consolation both to hear from his lips and to see put in practice the grand and holy maxims which are contained in his volume, so that what is written in these pages is but the expression of his thoughts and actions. I have read the work attentively. Everything in it, as far as I can judge, is calculated to edify, and full of the Spirit of God. The sentiments are noble and elevated, and on the whole, gives one a sublime conception of the religious life."
ETIENNE LE CAMUS, The Bishop of Grenoble (1681-1707) and Cardinal

No book within the memory of man has won for itself greater esteem at court, amongst the people, in the upper circles of society. But that would be little, if it had not at the same time produced inestimable fruits of virtue whereof I am myself a witness."
OLIVIER LEFÈVRE D'ORMESSON: magistrate and associate of Madame de Sévigné, Racine, Boileau, La Fontaine, Bossuet, Bourdaloue.

As to the results of its publication Bossuet wrote to de Rancé "The book has produced all the good effects I had anticipated. It has done great good everywhere. You ought to give thanks to God for giving you so happy an inspiration."

Back to Asceticism II: The Trappist Option

A Translation with Introduction and Notes of
DE LA SAINTETÉ ET DES DEVOIRS DE LA VIE MONASTIQUE

Armand-Jean de Rancé

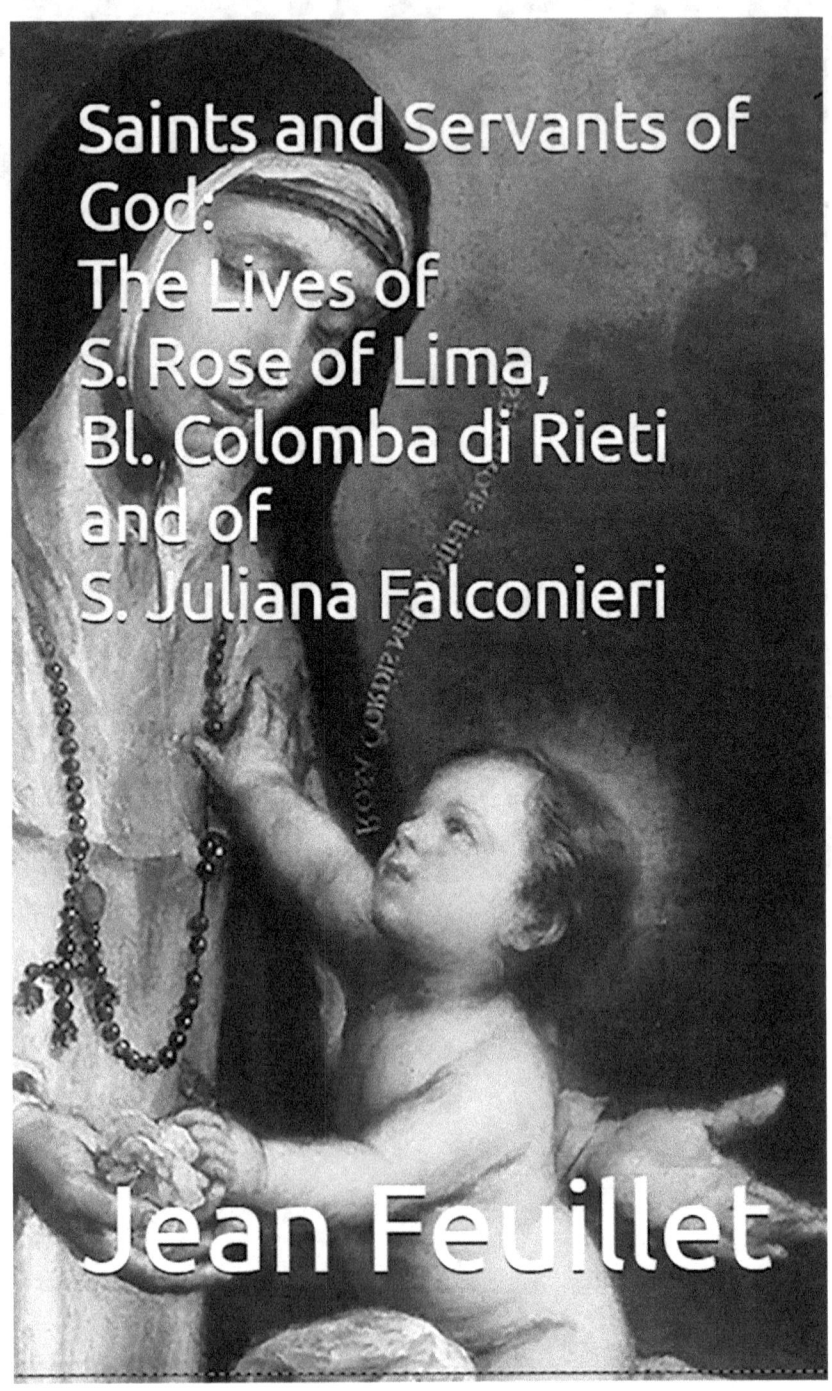

"English readers, who may not have been in the habit of reading the Lives of the Saints, and especially the authentic Processes of the Congregation of Sacred Rites, **may be a little startled with the Life of S. Rose.** The visible intermingling of the natural and supernatural worlds, which seems to increase as the saints approach through the grace of God to their first innocence, may even offend where persons have been in the habit of paring and batting down the "unearthly," in order to evade objections and lighten the load of the controversialist, rather than of meditating with awe and thankfulness and deep self-abasement on the wonders of God in His saints."
—Father Frederick Faber of the Oratory

Our re-typeset edition of this work, containing biographies of three third order saints—two Dominicans and one Servite—runs to 400 pages with 133 illustrations. At $22.50 on Amazon it is a wonderful bargain.

It might be you

Anecdotes of a Missionary

Peter Geiermann

It Might Be You is filled with 64 faith-building anecdotes perfect for reading together as a Catholic family as well as for private spiritual reading. Some are funny, some are sad and some are stranger than fiction. They are grace-filled episodes from the mission work of Fr. Peter Geiermann, who preached parish missions in many cities and towns throughout the midwest. Like a modern day Acts of the Apostles these anecdotes show the grace of God acting in the lives of ordinary people in the early twentieth century.

Very worthwhile, inspiring and memorable, this book is a keeper. It is an excellent gift for many occasions and a cherished addition to any Catholic's library. Who would part with it? Brighten up your library by ordering yours at once.

www.ingramcontent.com/pod-product-compliance
Lightning Source LLC
Chambersburg PA
CBHW051810230426
43672CB00012B/2677